PETER JONES

D0714239

Personally Speaking

The Principles and Power of Anointed Preaching and Teaching

Bob Gordon

Sovereign World

Sovereign World Ltd
PO Box 777
Tonbridge
Kent TN11 9XT
England

Copyright © 1995 Dr Bob Gordon

All rights reserved. No part of this publication may be reproduced, stored in a retrieval system or transmitted, in any form or by any means, electronic, mechanical, photocopying or otherwise, without the prior written consent of the publisher. Short extracts may be used for review purposes.

Bible quotations are taken from the NIV, The Holy Bible, New International Version. © Copyright 1973, 1978, 1984 International Bible Society. Published by Hodder & Stoughton.

AV – Authorised Version. Crown copyright

KJV – King James Version. Crown copyright

ISBN: 1 85240 153 2

Typeset by CRB Associates, Lenwade, Norwich
Printed in England by Clays Ltd, St. Ives plc.

*'Pray for me, that the Lord would give me houseroom
again to hold a candle to this dark world.'*

(Samuel Rutherford)

Preface

I have written this small book out of a sense of thanksgiving. It will soon become clear just how much I owe to preachers who have undertaken their task seriously yet joyously. I have written it also with a sense of conviction. My conviction is that preaching will again become central to our ministry in the power of the Spirit. The best converts are born from it, the best Christians grow out of it and the best miracles follow it. I offer it also in the hope that it will not only instruct but inspire others to take up the greatest calling in the world. The words of 2 Timothy 1:11, *'of this gospel I was appointed a herald and an apostle and a teacher'*, catch the mood of what I want to say.

My warm thanks go to two members of my team in particular who have aided and abetted the writing of *Personally Speaking*; namely, Anne Holmes and Sue Dixon. My thanks also to Chris Mungeam and the staff of Sovereign World for their encouragement and help in the process.

Bob Gordon
Norwich 1995

Contents

Chapter 1

A Personal Word

In one sense I owe my life to preaching. Right from the beginning of my Christian experience God has spoken powerfully into my life through the preaching ministry of other men. Some of these men I have heard at first hand, others I have only encountered through their writings or biographies. Nevertheless, the fact remains that through their preaching my life has been radically affected in so many significant ways. W.E. Sangster, the great Methodist preacher, once said that

> 'preaching is a constant agent of the divine power by which the greatest miracle God ever works is wrought again and again.'

Those who have felt the power of the Holy Spirit come into their lives through the ministry of preaching will know exactly what he means. Paul underlines the same truth when he says to the church at Corinth that

> *'God was pleased through the foolishness of what was preached to save those who believe.'* (1 Corinthians 1:21)

The older translation seems to suggest that it is the **act of preaching** which is foolish, *'through the foolishness of preaching'*, whereas, the New International Version more correctly reminds us that it is the message of the Gospel which seems foolish to unbelieving minds. There is a sense in which both are true. No preacher worth his salt will fail to admit that there have been times when what he is doing seems a foolish enterprise in the natural even to him. It is only by the anointing and power of the Holy Spirit that this foolish thing is transformed into the means by which God speaks with His voice into the hearts and minds of those who listen.

I was **birthed** in preaching. I mean by this that my personal spiritual experience began when God spoke to me through the words of an evangelist. Obviously, the Spirit of God had been at work in my life before that event. As the years have progressed in my own preaching ministry it has become more and more evident to me that it is often part of the preacher's privilege to reap where others have sown. This is especially true, I believe, in the ministry of the evangelist. We often give great credit to those who have drawn in the net through their evangelistic preaching without recognizing that their part came at the end of a sometimes long process of spiritual conviction and preparation by many different means in which the Holy Spirit was leading and guiding towards the moment of confession and commitment. Of course, we do need to thank God for every true evangelistic ministry and, indeed for every other faithful ministry of the word by which men and women are greatly affected in their lives as far as God is concerned. As I said, from the human point of view, I owe my Christian birth to a preacher. I can recall, as though it was yesterday, the effect of that word into my life although I was only twelve years of age at the time. I learned two lessons from that experience which have shaped my own view of the action of the word ever since. First, it was not so much the **actual words** the man was uttering which made an impact on me. Some of the words, as I remember, were already very familiar to me from the spiritual context within which I was nurtured. There was something more to it than that. There was a word within the words or behind the words. Surely this is the action of the

10

Holy Spirit bringing the revelation of God to bear on one's heart and mind. Second, when the man finished and I responded, he was not happy to accept a superficial or shallow response. He took me back to the Scriptures and pointed out again a specific word which the Spirit of God laid as a deposit into my life. These words are, in fact, found in Romans 10:9:

> *'If you confess with your mouth, "Jesus is Lord," and believe in your heart that God raised him from the dead, you will be saved.'*

I have always believed that this was an essential and important part of that early experience. This word was embedded by the Holy Spirit into my own spirit and through all those years has been the bedrock of my own ongoing experience in God.

I was **inspired** by preaching. A few years later, in my teenage years, I left home to work in a hospital in the west of Scotland. Those were formative but difficult years for me. At times I struggled hugely to keep my Christian faith and testimony alive. Yet even in those times God continued to speak to me. In particular, I began to have a pull in my heart towards the full-time ministry. This was very unusual because the spiritual context in which I had been nurtured was set against any idea of ordained ministry and within my own family there were strong feelings against any such idea. In fact, I had hardly ever been inside a traditional church in my life. Nevertheless, I found these ideas forming in my mind and I can remember once paying a visit to the minister of a nearby parish church to speak with him about the matter. The major influence in my life at this formative time came from two very different, but equally powerful sources. They were sources that were foreign to my upbringing and, as far as I remember, I was introduced to them through some patients and friends I met in the hospital who came from a wider Christian background than myself. Both sources were preachers.

On the one hand I was magnetised by the sermons and biography of Peter Marshall[1]. As I read his words I could almost hear him speak although I never heard him in the flesh. His words inspired me, I could feel the power of them. There was a quality about his preaching that I had never met before. Although I was reading his sermons I felt that I could see in my mind the scenes about which he spoke. His gift seemed to be to make these things live in the imagination of his hearers and, no doubt, his readers. Of course, he had come from my part of Scotland before emigrating to America in the earlier part of the century. There he had become well known as an effective preacher and had risen to become the minister of one of the most important churches of the day as well as being appointed Chaplain to the US Senate. No doubt all of this added interest and colour to everything I read. But as I devoured books like *Mr Jones, Meet The Master*[2] I found, like Wesley had said, my heart strangely warmed. It was as though, through this preacher, God was prising me loose from a narrower and, perhaps, more restricted arena, and preparing my heart for a call that was far outside anything I had known or imagined.

On the other hand I was equally impressed by the sermons and writings of a great English preacher, Dr W.E. Sangster of Westminster. Both of these men came from a generation immediately before my own. Sangster had become famous as a preacher in London during the Second World War and was one of a number of well known and influential preachers of his time. He again, had a certain personal flair. I have only ever heard him preach live in a recording but that only served to confirm my feelings of the spiritual stature of this man of God. Over the years which followed, his sermons and writings became the main influence in my developing Christian life. I think that it was through the preaching of Sangster that I was most influenced towards the idea of entering the ordained ministry. In the next few years that followed through my early twenties, it was the ministry of Sangster which most inspired and affected my own life and developing ministry. During this period I had moved to England to serve

in the Royal Air Force and subsequently I spent a few years
in business. I preached a great deal in Methodist churches in
this period. A fact, no doubt, which grew out of my inward
admiration for the man God had used to speak so much to
me. Some tried to influence me towards becoming a Methodist minister but I knew in my heart this would never be. I still
have all the books of Sangster and Marshall on my book-
shelves but the time came when I saw so clearly that God
needed to develop my own ministry and style. I will ever be
grateful, however, for the inspirational influence of these
great servants of God on my life.

I was **convicted** by preaching. After a few years in business
I began to feel the stirring of God more and more in my
spirit. I knew that ultimately God was calling me to commit
myself in a full-time sense to the ministry of the word. In
fact, my wife and I still laugh at the memory of our first
date years before when I intimated to her on our first night
out together that she would have to be prepared to enter full-
time ministry. She was totally willing for it then and she has
continued with that same willing and open spirit ever since.
But that is another story.

The crunch came one year when we were taken to visit the
Keswick convention. I had no real intention of going to
many of the convention meetings but it turned out to be one
of those occasions when God has a greater say in the matter.
On the Friday night at the end of the week, as I remember it,
we went to a meeting which had the aim of encouraging
people to respond to serve God in some sort of full-time
ministry. The preacher was George Duncan, at that time
minister of St. George's Tron, a famous evangelical Church
of Scotland in Glasgow. He took as his text words from the
Epistle of James in the Authorised Version:

*'Therefore, to him that knoweth to do good, and doeth it
not, to him it is sin.'*   (James 4:17)

The words went home to my heart like an arrow. For the
past few years I had known the testimony of God in my own

spirit. At last He had brought me right to the point of decision. When it came to the end of the address George Duncan made an appeal for response. My wife and I found ourselves on our feet in a moment, confirming what turned out to be the most momentous decision of our lives. It was a decision which made a great impact on my business career and which is the source of everything that has happened in my life ever since. It is a decision, I would want to say, that I would make all over again because for all the aggravations and challenges we have faced over the years the conviction of that call has never gone away. It has been the foundation and bulwark of all our experience although it has had to be worked out in a number of interesting and different dimensions.

I was **motivated** by preaching. Eventually I found myself studying at theological college for what was then the Congregational ministry. My Old Testament professor was a Welshman called Edgar Jones, who eventually became Principal of the college. He had an incredible love for the Old Testament and he fired my own spirit as far as the study of Hebrew was concerned. Above all, however, he was a preacher; an amazing communicator who could make the Scriptures, in particular the Old Testament, live. I don't think he would have described himself as an evangelical but he certainly had an evangelical spirit. His commitment to communicating the word in a personal and relevant way was evident to all who heard him and he left an indelible mark on my own spirit as far as preaching was concerned. His preaching fired and motivated me. I saw someone, who although an academic, had as the basis of his life a call to preach. Another man whom I came to know quite well and who manifested the same balance was Professor Kingsley Barrett of Durham University. A brilliant academician whose greatest joy, nevertheless, was to preach in the open air in the middle of town every Easter to proclaim the resurrection power of Christ.

I was **challenged** by preaching. I was ordained in 1971 and for the first year or two of my ministry things went pretty

well. I had been inducted as minister of a small Congregational (afterwards United Reformed) Church in the city of
Durham. I was also appointed to the chaplaincy team in the
university and started working towards a PhD in the Depart-
ment of Theology. As time went on, however, I began to feel
an increasing unease and dissatisfaction about my ministry.
On the outside it was fine, the church grew and changed
quite radically. I found myself accepted in all the other areas
of life. Yet something was happening which presented me
with a great challenge. The phenomenon known as charismatic renewal had hit town. It started in a high Anglican
church across the valley from my own. Many people were
affected by this new move of God and a church which had
been dead in tradition began to show signs of new life and
growth. Amongst the student population hundreds of young
people became Christians and joined in this new move. It
became quite a talking point amongst the chaplains who, in
the main were irritated by it. For myself, I began to be challenged first, by the needs I saw around me in the lives of
many students and second, by a growing awareness that all
my theological expertise seemed unable to meet that need.

The crunch came early in 1974 when I was asked by a
good friend and colleague to attend a conference in Scotland
run by an organisation known as the Fountain Trust. The
Fountain Trust had been started in the early sixties by
Michael Harper, an Anglican minister to encourage spiritual
renewal throughout the churches. It was an important cata-
lyst for the move of the Holy Spirit which subsequently
affected every denomination and church group to some
degree or other. This was a special conference for clergy. At
first I was reluctant to attend because I knew the leanings of
the Fountain Trust and I was not very warm towards their
theology at that time. However, after some time I decided to
take up the offer and found myself some time later with
thirty or so other ministers at the event.

As the conference proceeded I found myself impressed by
the spirit of it. No one was pushy or aggressive; it seemed as
though there was a genuine concern to help. The final

evening of the conference arrived; it was the penultimate meeting. The conference was to end the next morning with a communion service. A speaker had been invited, an Anglican priest called Harold Parks. As soon as he began to speak I felt an empathy with his spirit. He was a man who centred his ideas on the Scriptures and had an evident maturity in the things of God. It was as he continued to speak, however, that I really felt the impact of what he was saying. He read and spoke from Isaiah 6:1–8, the account of Isaiah's vision of the glory of God. I have rarely seen a man so translucent; it seemed as though the word shone through him. When he spoke of the glory of God and the sense of the holiness of God it felt as though the living hand of God was stretched out on me at that moment. I have never forgotten the impact of those words which were squeezed from the lips of the prophet. The pathos of them is best felt in the older King James version:

> *'Woe is me! for I am undone; because I am a man of unclean lips, and I dwell in the midst of a people of unclean lips: for mine eyes have seen the King, the* LORD *of hosts.'*

When he finished speaking everyone else left the room and went downstairs to have a warm drink. I discovered that I could not physically move. It was as though all the strength had gone out of my arms and legs. I felt as though I was experiencing the same sort of thing that Isaiah himself had gone through. I had a tremendous sense of the glory and awe of God's presence. If I had felt dark before through a sense of spiritual depression it was nothing compared with the darkness I now felt in my spirit as it was exposed to the overpowering light of God. The Holy Spirit had taken the spoken words of the preacher and turned them into reality in my own being. Even after more than twenty years I can say that it was easily the most challenging and profound moment of spiritual awareness of my whole Christian experience.

Eventually someone came back upstairs to find me because my presence had obviously been missed at supper. In fact, two men had come back. One, the friend who had taken me, the other Michael Harper, leader of the conference. They said nothing, or at least nothing I remember. I think they prayed for me to be released from the hold of this overpowering weakness and let me go with them downstairs. They gave me something to drink but I was barely able to hold the mug. I went to bed with the same trembling feeling not quite knowing whether I was alive or dead.

Next morning I rose early and as I drew the curtains back the sun streamed into my room. It was as though the Son of Righteousness had risen with healing in His wings! This was my first experience of the living power and presence of the Holy Spirit. It was an experience which was to have radical consequences over the years and still continues to do so. It is an experience which wrote my theology of the Spirit for me and one which makes me so discontent with many of the more trivial theories I see around me today.

I am **concerned about** preaching. It will come as no surprise after all that I have shared to learn that preaching is now the main interest of my life. Sometimes I feel as though I was born behind my time; the day for preaching of the sort I have been describing seems to have passed in many places. I believe, however, that there is not only a need for a revival of spiritual communication with this power and content, but that we are on the verge of another move of God in this regard. There needs to be a trumpet sound! This small book is meant to encourage those who read it to prepare themselves for this event; it is meant to encourage and stimulate. The major focus of this book is more on the spiritual dynamics of communication in the Spirit of God than all the small details of practical things. We need to grasp again the sense of awe that men of God experience when they realise that it is God who is speaking through them. We need to capture again a sense of urgency concerning the gospel and the revelation truth of God. People's taste needs to be developed for that which will build up their faith and bring strength into their inner being. We need to focus more on what God has to say than on what we think. Of course, there are all sorts of preachers and preaching. There are others who bring God's word in less orthodox styles and means. There is a need for the truly prophetic to be released among us to overpower the false and the shallow. Fewer little pictures of tinkling waterfalls are needed and more revelation words from God which bear within them all the hallmarks of authenticity from the throne of God.

There are many different sorts of preaching. It's not my intention at the moment to look at every single different style but I believe there are some aspects of spiritual communication that we urgently need to encourage today. For example:

We need **expository preaching**. This is preaching which is based on and regulated by a study of the Scriptures. It expounds the truth of the Scripture. I want to make a plea for a revival of expository preaching. Unfortunately it has become identified in people's minds with dullness and boredom. It should not be like that at all. One of my own best memories of preaching was when I did an expository study on the Epistle of James. Before that time I had loved and preached on different parts of the book but it wasn't until I expounded James from beginning to end that I realised the tremendous dynamism and relevance of this brief epistle at the end of the New Testament. Great benefit can be gained through getting into the habit of expounding the Scriptures and leading people into the riches and life that come from a systematic exegesis of the word of God. It doesn't have to be dull and dry. In fact, if it is then I would say that it is not true exposition of the word of God in Scripture.

We need proper **didactic preaching**, preaching which is meant to instruct, in which the true role of the spiritual teacher comes into its own within the Body of Christ. Teaching does not only mean expounding Scripture; it is the systematic presentation of principles and biblical ideas which control and affect how people think in relation to the things of God. When the Holy Spirit teaches us and leads us,

He shows us what to do, what is appropriate, what is right. Didactic preaching aims to provide guidelines for living and to give insight into issues of Christian belief. This is one area where clarity is so much needed today. People need to get a hold of divine principles otherwise they will have neither foundation nor guidance for life. Didactic preaching delivers people from fuzzy thinking and helps them see clearly what they believe in relation to the great principles of faith and life.

We need **devotional preaching**, through which the hearts of God's people are drawn more closely to Himself. Its purpose is to draw them into a deeper knowledge of God and of themselves. If this preaching is done really effectively then people's hearts will be moved by 'a godly theme'. I believe that one of the most motivational realities for a Christian audience is when their hearts are stirred through the power of a word like this. Through the warmth and depth of a devotional address all the baggage and needs of a person's life can be taken away as they are led from the outside of their lives into the inner sanctum of the presence of God.

We need **evangelistic preaching**. I think that evangelistic preaching is one of the greatest challenges of all. Some imagine that it is easy; all we need, they say, is a few anec- dotes together with a word of testimony. There is no doubt that personal testimony can be very important in evangelistic communication because it relates the word to life and pro- vides a living illustration of truth to those who are listening which otherwise might be quite foreign to their ears and hearts. There is much more to good evangelistic preaching than this, however, and as long as we persist in living with superficial ideas about it the job will never be fulfilled in any worthwhile sense. Every time I am asked to be involved in evangelism I feel a great challenge of spirit because I feel I am called to take the great central mysteries of the Christian faith and speak them in such a way that their truth will penetrate into the minds and hearts of those who listen. It takes a special gift to make profound things clear and the best evangelists are those who are able to speak out of a deep understanding of the faith while, at the same time, making it seem so simple that a rank outsider can hear the message clear and plain.

We need **prophetic preaching**. All preaching is, of course, in some sense prophetic. There is, however, a sort of declaration that carries an urgency and comes with a relevant cutting edge which stands apart from every other kind of spiritual communication.

Prophetic preaching is different too from the practice of bringing 'prophetic words' in a meeting. It is more of a statement made with the urgency of the Holy Spirit which creates awareness in the hearer and a sense of urgency in the heart.

Prophetic preaching finds its impetus from a number of different sources. It can, for example, be inspired by reflection on a known state of affairs in a church or nation. The word of God is mingled with this awareness to bring a divine perspective to bear on the situation and perhaps lead the hearers in a specific direction or action.

On the other hand this sort of preaching can come with powerful spontaneity and immediacy. With no previous knowledge of events or situations the Spirit of God can cause the speaker to bring a message through direct revelation which speaks right into the heart of the situation.

We need **apologetic preaching**. In this context the word apologetic does not mean that we are saying that we are sorry about something. Here the word is used in a technical sense of making a defense for something or a case on behalf of something. In relation to the gospel it does not mean that we apologise for the gospel; rather the opposite. A famous scholar called A.B. Bruce put it simply and well when he said that 'apologetics is Christianity defensively stated.'

The words of 1 Peter 3:15 remind us of the importance of this task:

> *'In your hearts set apart Christ as Lord. Always be prepared to give an answer to everyone who asks you to give the reason for the hope that you have.'*

In the chapters which follow we will explore some of the spiritual principles and practical steps which are involved in all effective spiritual communication.

References

1. Marshall, Peter. 1954. *Mr Jones, Meet The Master*. Collins Fontana Books
2. *Ibid*

Chapter 2

Oracles of God

The word preaching bores most people who don't really know what it's meant to be about. The image of fusty churches and irrelevant homilies has given rise to the notion that preaching is an outdated and outmoded way of communicating that has little, if any, relevance in the modern world. Some contemporary attempts at the art only convince people that preaching is nothing but a rambling, somewhat disconnected series of ideas which may or may not benefit those who hear them.

I looked up a dictionary to find out what it had to say about the matter. Its definitions seemed to reflect the sort of mood I have just described. It did admit that preaching involved making something known but the main emphasis of the definition left one with the idea of something formal, stiff and boring that was only usually carried out by clerics. In fact one defined a preacher as 'especially a Protestant clergyman'! The most common emphasis of all the definitions seemed to lie within the field of earnest moral and religious advice. No wonder our minds have been biased away from, what for the New Testament is, a vital testimony to the presence, power and promise of the Kingdom of God.

The Essentials

When we turn to the pages of the New Testament we are confronted with a very different view of preaching. Here it is not seen as something irrelevant but revelational. It is not seen as something dry and dull but full of living power because it is the carrier wave of the Kingdom. Through preaching in the power of God men and women are brought into direct contact with the living word of God and with the reality of His kingdom on earth. In fact, Paul, one of the greatest exponents of this ministry, poses the question:

> 'How can they hear without someone preaching to them? And how can they preach unless they are sent? As it is written, "How beautiful are the feet of those who bring good news!"' (Romans 10:14, 15)

Two major terms are used in the New Testament to express the heart of what preaching is all about.
1. The first and main word that the New Testament writers use to describe this activity carries within it a sense of vibrancy and urgency. It is the word *'kerusso'*. A *'kerux'* was a herald, someone who announced momentous news. Someone who came with a sense of urgency, someone who was a representative of a power greater than himself. The *'kerugma'* was his message: it was what he proclaimed: it described the content of his proclamation. This was not some dispassionate or disinterested discourse. The man was bearing news. It was not his own, it had been given to him!

Such is the power of this word *'kerusso'*. It means to 'announce, summon, declare'. In the case of the New Testament the declaration was concerning the Kingdom of God. We can see this most clearly in the experience of Jesus. As He sets out on His mission we can almost feel the sense of call and commitment along with the feeling that we are watching something happening to one whose time has arrived. That is precisely what Jesus claimed. Matthew gives us the report in words that highlight the sense of the significance of the moment:

> *'When Jesus heard that John had been put in prison he returned to Galilee. Leaving Nazareth, he went and lived in Capernaum, which was by the lake in the area of Zebulun and Naphtali – to fulfil what was said through the prophet Isaiah:*
> *"Land of Zebulun and land of Naphtali,*
>   *the way to the sea, along the Jordan,*
>   *Galilee of the Gentiles –*
> *the people living in darkness*
>   *have seen a great light;*
> *on those living in the land of the shadow of death*
>   *a light has dawned."*
> *From that time on Jesus began to preach, "Repent, for the kingdom of heaven is near."'*   (Matthew 4:12–17)

These words vibrate with life and vitality. At the heart they carry three important elements. **Firstly**, a sense of purpose. *'Leaving Nazareth, he went and lived in Capernaum.'*

The words seem to convey something more than just a casual event – this wasn't just a whim, it wasn't just a case of 'let's pack up our bags, it's time to go'. He was driven ... He was motivated ... There was a call in His heart from His Father. Jesus went and lived in Capernaum – not just the description of a geographical location, but the statement of a deep spiritual motivation.

Secondly, a sense of fulfilment ... *'to fulfil what was said through the prophet Isaiah.'*

Some writers would have us believe that Matthew merely included these words from the old prophet Isaiah as a suitable quotation for the purpose of the account. I don't think so. These words capture in a profound and meaningful way the sense of call that pervaded the heart and mind of Jesus. Everything that Jesus did served a purpose. His purpose in leaving Nazareth was to fulfil the words of the prophet

Isaiah. This was the beginning of an important phase in the life and ministry of Jesus because –

> *'From that time on Jesus began to preach . . .'*

The words which follow betray for us **the third significant element**, namely, a sense of urgency ... *'the kingdom of heaven is near.'*

Someone has put it rather nicely:

> 'The essence of preaching for the New Testament is not the method or style of delivery, nor even the one who heralds or preaches, but the message of truth itself.'
>
> (*Complete Biblical Library*)

You see it is what is proclaimed that is important. This is the depth of the meaning of this word *'kerusso'*. It is about preaching; it is about announcing; it is about declaring! But it is primarily about what is declared. When we ask the question as to what was declared the answer is the presence and reality of the Kingdom of God.

Paul emphasizes the very same point. In 1 Corinthians 1:21 he says:

> *'God was pleased through the foolishness of what was preached to save those who believe.'*   (NIV)

Right at the beginning of chapter one, I noted the apparent tension between the New International Version and the King James Version of this text. It is worth repeating here. The Authorised Version reads:

> *'It pleased God through the foolishness of preaching to save them who believe.'*

This might give the impression that the important thing was the act of preaching when, in fact, the proper meaning of the original is more truly reflected in the NIV rendering which puts the emphasis on the content of what is preached. Here the stress is not on the style of delivery but the power of the message. Paul underlines this when he says again to the believers in Corinth:

> *'When I came to you ... I did not come with eloquence or superior wisdom ... I came to you in weakness and fear, and with much trembling. My message and my preaching were not with wise and persuasive words, but with a demonstration of the Spirit's power, so that your faith might not rest on men's wisdom, but on God's power.'*
>
> (1 Corinthians 2:1–5)

The emphasis must be on the content. Then the hearers' faith will be in the power of God and not in the persuasion of man. However, this will only be so when the preacher 'knows' what he's going to preach. Not just in the sense that he's worked it out beforehand, but that he has a first-hand, intimate knowledge of the truth of the message. As Jesus said, *'If you abide in my word ... you shall know the truth.'* Sadly, this is one reason why there has been such a discount in preaching over the last thirty years. The church at large does not have a personal knowledge of the truth. It has been riddled with uncertainty at a biblical and theological level. How can people know what to preach if they don't know what they believe?

The depth of this word *'kerusso'* emphasizes that the men who went to preach (including Jesus) absolutely and undoubtedly knew what they believed. There was no shadow of doubt as to what they were to do – they came to proclaim that the Kingdom of God was at hand.

2. **The second great word in the New Testament** is the word *'didasko'*. If we translate this straight into English it means 'to teach'. Again we might be in danger of imagining something dull, systematic or dead – something that you might not want to listen to. But, as we have seen already with *'kerusso'*, there is a depth of meaning and vitality in the Greek language which is missing in the English. As far as the

New Testament is concerned *'didasko'* expresses teaching that has within it the breath of life. The two words complement each other in this way: the fundamental emphasis of *'kerusso'* is the announcement of the breakthrough of God's Kingdom – it's here! The fundamental aspect of *'didasko'* is to show the way of life in God's Kingdom – this is what it means!

When we look at the men and women who preached in the New Testament we see that *'didasko'* interlinks with *'kerusso'* in just this way.

It is used of Jesus in the Gospels:

> *'Jesus went throughout Galilee, teaching in their synagogues, preaching the good news of the kingdom.'*
> (Matthew 4:23)

> *'Teacher, ... we know that you are a man of integrity and that you teach the way of God in accordance with the truth.'*   (Matthew 22:16)

It is used of the Apostles in the book of Acts:

> *'They arrested the apostles and put them in the public jail. But during the night an angel of the Lord opened the doors of the jail and brought them out. "Go stand in the temple courts," he said, "and tell the people the full message of this new life."*
>
> *At daybreak they entered the temple courts, as they had been told, and began to teach the people.'*
> (Acts 5:18–21)

This was a dynamic experience in the life of the early church. God brought them out and told them to *'teach the people'*. What did they teach them? They taught them *'the full message of this new life'*.

If you were to ask me what the substance of preaching and teaching is, I would say it is this: 'the announcement of the new life and the full message of the new life.'

It is true that in some of the Epistles, which reflect a later stage in the experience of the church, the word *'didasko'* becomes more formalised and takes on a sense of 'doctrine'. In the Epistle to Titus the office of an overseer in the church is described in the following way:

> *'Since an overseer is entrusted with God's work ... He must hold firmly to the trustworthy message as it has been taught, so that he can encourage others by sound doctrine and refute those who oppose it.'* (Titus 1:7, 9)

Another element has been added that isn't present in the word *'kerusso'*. We notice that Paul talks of *'sound doctrine'*. Here we have an understanding of this word 'teach' speaking of that which has been passed on as being the deposit of truth.

Titus is instructed to *'refute those who oppose it'*. *'Didasko'* is not so much a declaration of the arrival of the Kingdom, it includes apologetics, that is, a defence of the truth. It provides a defence and an offensive against those who are propagating error. This is a very important element of preaching and teaching for the New Testament writers. Not only is there the declaration of initial truth, but it comes against untruth.

The Call

I once had an old friend in East Yorkshire. He lived in a little house in a small village and his main purpose and joy in life was to keep the Methodist church running. He never preached himself, but gave hospitality to visiting ministers. Often probationer preachers newly arrived on the local Methodist circuit would be sent to him. These were rookies just out of college. The superintendent knew that my friend would assess these young men very quickly and no doubt would tell them how he felt they measured up as preachers. The habit was for the preacher to take both afternoon and evening services in the small village chapel and between times to have tea with my friend and his wife.

One Sunday a young man came to preach. As they sat talking between the afternoon and evening services, over tea and scones, the subject turned to preaching. 'Young man' says my friend to this young Methodist preacher, 'dost thou reckon that God has called thee?' (This is how he often spoke) 'Because I don't reckon He's even whistled on thee!'

This is something that may be difficult for some of us to get to grips with today. In the New Testament preaching is not just something done out of fancy or good intention, it is the result of a deep sense of 'must': a call of God, which urges us to pay attention to the inner movements of our spirit and the rising awareness of the power of God's word in our hearts and minds.

This view of preaching and teaching is impressed on Timothy by his spiritual father in God:

> *'Devote yourself to the public reading of Scripture, to preaching and to teaching. Do not neglect your gift, which was given you through a prophetic message when the body of elders laid hands on you.'*
>
> (1 Timothy 4:13–15)

Again, when Paul writes to the Corinthians he expresses much the same point of view. He expresses the sense of compulsion that any genuine preacher will know at times.

> *'I am compelled to preach. Woe to me if I do not preach the gospel.'* (1 Corinthians 9:16)

We can very clearly feel the sense of 'must' which carried Paul along in his communication of the gospel. It is essential, if we are going to have vital preaching brought back into the Church today, that a generation of called servants is raised up who feel that 'sense of must' laid upon them by the Spirit of God.

The whole New Testament seems to witness to the need

for this sense of commission as we preach the word of God. Paul expresses it so clearly in Romans 10:15:

> *'How can they preach unless they are sent?'*

Likewise he says elsewhere:

> *'In Christ we speak before God with sincerity, like men sent from God.'*   (2 Corinthians 2:17)

Where are the preachers and teachers today who will answer the call of God? Where are those who have that burning compulsion in their hearts to be sent out to deliver God's truth to a hungry people?

The Preacher

I have on my shelves a thirteen volume set on *Twenty Centuries of Great Preaching.*[1] It ends in 1971. I have often wondered how many 'greats' we could add to the list from the past twenty years. It is true that in countries like the United States many books on the subject have been written over the past few decades but in Britain most of the significant works come from the experience and pen of preachers of the past.

This fact is illustrated when we note some of the most popular works of a recent generation. We could name books like *Heralds of God*[2] by Dr James S. Stewart (original 1946) or *The Craft of the Sermon*[3] (1954) by the great Methodist preacher Dr W.E. Sangster. Dr Martin Lloyd Jones has been described as 'the last of the preachers'. I pray that this may prove to be a misguided prophecy. However, his book *Preachers and Preaching*[4] (1971) has been a gold-mine for those who long to follow in his footsteps. More recently, Dr D.W. Cleverley-Ford has produced a number of books on the subject, notably *Preaching Today*[5] (1969).

This book is interesting in that it is written from within the boundaries of a Church that has suffered all the impact of liberalism. It is a good book, but it highlights one of the reasons why preaching has diminished over the last thirty years. The attack by liberalism on the confidence of the gospel has brought about a failure of nerve as far as preaching is concerned. Nobody is quite sure what they can say with confidence. The impact of the most negative aspects of biblical criticism has led in many quarters to the feeling that every statement must be surrounded by so many qualifications that it becomes hardly worth making them. This is the mood of a church infected by a liberal spirit. Who knows what to preach if the foundations are so weak? How can we be heralds if we don't know what we herald?

> *'If the trumpet does not sound a clear call, who will get ready for battle?'* (1 Corinthians 14:8)

It is also a fact that the context in which the preacher must communicate the gospel today has changed dramatically. Over the last 30 years charismatic renewal has changed the face of the church. The preacher today has to take on board a lot more challenges than the minister in a context of more traditional church preaching. We really have got to learn the craft of preaching again from the Holy Spirit. This, of course, is a very exciting prospect! If we understand the meaning of *'kerusso'* and *'didasko'* and submit to the power of the Spirit in our lives, we too can discover the heartland of preaching again.

W.E. Sangster, one of the greatest preachers of the twentieth century, said of Billy Graham's preaching:

> 'Homiletically his sermons leave almost everything to be desired. They are often without discernible structure. Sometimes with little or no logical progression. Yet in the wake of this "poor" preaching I have seen things happen I never expected to see, things which I doubt any man has seen since the Day of Pentecost.'[6]

Tom Allan, one of the best communicators Scotland has seen, said much the same thing about Billy Graham:

> 'His sermons were often without form. There were some quirks in his grammar ... But for myself it was preaching in the New Testament sense of the word. It was "proclamation of the faith once delivered to the saints" ... The verdict simply is: "We understand what this man is saying." ' [7]

What significant words! – 'preaching in the New Testament sense'. Of course, this doesn't give us a licence to be sloppy. Martin Lloyd Jones has said:

> 'To me the work of preaching is the highest and the greatest and the most glorious calling to which anyone can ever be called.' [8]

This is what both the church and the world needs today. Servants of the word who are called by God and empowered by the Holy Spirit:
- To proclaim the words of God's truth.
- To show, by living instruction and example, that the Kingdom of God has come among us.
- To declare that the time for confusion and uncertainty is passed.

True heralds, preaching words of reality from a living God. I believe we are soon going to see a new call for just such proclamation in the Body of Jesus Christ. People can only go on with water for so long, until they start to die of malnutrition. At that time they will call in desperation for those who will preach and teach the Living Bread of the Word of God.

The Essence

When Paul asks the question in Romans 10:14: *'How can they hear without someone preaching to them?'* he is highlighting another important aspect of this great ministry of preaching. Preaching is proclamation through a person. In Mark's Gospel, we have the account of the man who was healed from a legion of demonic spirits. Afterwards he wanted to go with Jesus, but instead he was told:

> ' *"Go home to your family and tell them how much the Lord has done for you and how he has had mercy on you." So the man went away and began to tell in the Decapolis how much Jesus had done for him. And all the people were amazed.'*   (Mark 5:19, 20)

The man went away and told people. He didn't send a report about it, he went himself and told the people in the ten cities of all that Jesus had done for him – and they were amazed! There are two sides to effective spiritual communication. It is a coming together of God's Word, given by the Holy Spirit, on the one hand, and on the other, the personality, gifting and abilities of a human being.

One other strand of New Testament witness bears testimony to the same fact. Time and again Paul speaks in impersonal terms with regard to the gospel. Of course, he recognises powerfully that the gospel does not come from man and that the centre of it is Jesus.

As he says in Romans 1:9 ' *... with my whole heart in preaching the gospel of his Son... '* That's what the gospel is – the gospel of God's Son. Yet in the next chapter, he says *'as my gospel declares'* (Romans 2:16), and two or three times in his letters he uses those astounding words *'my gospel'*. What does Paul mean? Has he invented a gospel that's different from anyone else's gospel? Has he invented a gospel that's different from that of Jesus? Is he coming with a new, 'cultist' revelation? Hardly – it's the very thing that he speaks against in Galatians:

> *'If anybody is preaching to you a gospel other than what you accepted, let him be eternally condemned!'*
>   (Galatians 1:9)

So what does he mean by 'my gospel'? We see the answer in Romans 16:25:

> *'Now to him who is able to establish you by my gospel and the proclamation of Jesus Christ.'*

It is not a new gospel. It's that same gospel of God, but it has been made real in Paul by the inward workings of the Holy Spirit. He has taken it to himself as his possession from God, to proclaim it in the power of the Holy Spirit. No preacher can ever preach the gospel, unless in a deep personal way they have taken hold of what Paul describes as 'my gospel'. We are not giving lectures, we are not delivering sermons or homilies – we are passionately and personally involved in the preaching. That is our task.

A wonderful story which illustrates the point so clearly is told by the great preacher, James Stewart. About 300 years ago an English merchant visited Scotland from London. During his travels, he went around different towns in Scotland, listening to 'great preachers of the day'. When he went back to London, he reported what he had heard to his friends. This is what he said:

> 'At St. Andrews I listened to Robert Blair. That man showed me the Majesty of God. Afterwards, I heard a little fair man preaching' (Samuel Rutherford). 'That man showed me the Loveliness of Christ. Then I went to the town of Irvine and I heard a well-favoured old man; his name was David Dixon. That man showed me all my heart.'[9]

These words surely demonstrate the essential purpose of preaching:

– to show the Majesty of God;
– to show the Loveliness of Christ;
– to show all my heart.

If all our preaching struck these three chords or any of them we would be far richer for the experience.

Recently I came across some words written by the late Archbishop, William Temple. In their original setting they refer to worship, but could just as easily describe the power of preaching:

'To worship God is to quicken the conscience by the Holiness of God, to feed the mind with the Truth of God, to open the heart to the Love of God, to devote the will to the Purpose of God.' [10]

If we change the word 'worship' for 'preach', these words contain everything we've been considering. **When the word of God is preached in truth and power:**

The Holy Spirit quickens the conscience of the hearer –

'The word of God is living and active. Sharper than any double-edged sword, it penetrates even to dividing soul and spirit, joints and marrow; it judges the thoughts and attitudes of the heart.' (Hebrews 4:12)

God's truth feeds the mind –

'Be transformed by the renewing of your mind.'
(Romans 12:2)

God's love softens the heart –

'I pray that you ... may have power ... to grasp how wide and long and high and deep is the love of Christ, and to know this love that surpasses knowledge.'
(Ephesians 3:17, 18)

Our response to the living Word is to devote the will –

'Brothers, what shall we do?'
'Repent and be baptised, every one of you.'
(Acts 2:37, 38)

Preaching is not just words with no effect, it is something that fulfils an aim. The aim is that people will devote their hearts and minds and wills to the power of God.

In *Preaching Today* Dr Cleverley-Ford says these important words:

> 'The Church which poses as an amateur psychiatrist or an amateur welfare worker is bound to be superseded by the State-supported expert. The ministry of the Word is the Church's peculiar work, which in part gives her ministers their proper function.' [11]

Our job is to do this 'peculiar' work – the ministry of the Word.

> 'O Thou who camest from above
> The pure celestial fire to impart,
> Kindle a flame of sacred love
> On the mean altar of my heart.
>
> Jesus confirm my heart's desire
> To work and speak and think for Thee.
> Still let me guard the holy fire
> And still stir up Thy gift in me.'

(Charles Wesley)

References

1. Fant, C.E. Jr, Pinson, W.E. Jr and Hammer, D.E. (research associate). 1971. *Twenty Centuries of Great Preaching* (13 vol. series). Word Inc.
2. Stewart, James. 1955. *Heralds of God*. English University Press Ltd by arrangement with Hodder & Stoughton. (Re-issued as *Preaching*; part of a series in the 'Teach Yourself' books.)
3. Sangster, W.E. 1954. *The Craft of the Sermon*. Epworth Press
4. Lloyd Jones, Martyn. 1971. *Preachers and Preaching*. Hodder & Stoughton
5. Cleverley-Ford, D.W. 1969. *Preaching Today*. Epworth Press and SPCK
6. Fant, C.E. Jr, Pinson, W.E. Jr and Hammer D.E. (research associate). 1971. *Twenty Centuries of Great Preaching* (13 vol. series). Word Inc.

7. Fant, C.E. Jr, Pinson, W.E. Jr and Hammer, D.E. (research associate). 1971. *Twenty Centuries of Great Preaching* (13 vol. series). Word Inc.
8. Lloyd Jones, Martyn. 1971. *Preachers and Preaching*. Hodder & Stoughton
9. Stewart, James. 1955. *Heralds of God*. English University Press Ltd by arrangement with Hodder & Stoughton. (Re-issued as *Preaching*; part of a series in the 'Teach Yourself' books.)
10. Fant, C.E. Jr, Pinson, W.E. Jr and Hammer D.E. (research associate). 1971. *Twenty Centuries of Great Preaching* (13 vol. series). Word Inc.
11. Cleverley-Ford, D.W. 1969. *Preaching Today*. Epworth Press and SPCK

Chapter 3

The Ministry of the Word

The title of this chapter is almost a direct crib from that of a book by Watchman Nee called *The Ministry of God's Word*[1]. I came across this book in a surprising and unexpected way. On one occasion I was staying overnight at the home of an old friend and colleague in Edinburgh. He and his wife had kindly foregone the comfort of their own bedroom to give me rest. I was lying in bed about to go to sleep when my eyes began to wander up and down the rows of books in the bookcase opposite the bed. Suddenly my eye lit on this book by Watchman Nee. I had read some of his other writings but had never come across this particular volume. At the time I was preparing to make some video recordings on the subject of preaching and so the title instantly took my attention.

As I began to scan the book I felt a rising excitement in my spirit because here, I felt, was someone who was expressing in his own words many of the things I had been feeling deep within my own heart. As you read on you will discover that this book made quite an impact on my thinking, confirming many of my own thoughts and experiences and clarifying other aspects of the subject that his greater experience in the things of God enabled him to grasp and explain much more clearly than I could.

The words which follow were the very first words to arrest

my attention and make their impact on my mind. I meditated on them a great deal and can still recall the power of
the first impression on my soul.

> 'We learn from the Bible that God has a prime work to
> perform on earth which is to utter His word. If the word
> of God is taken away then almost nothing is left of
> God's work. No word, no work. When the word of
> God is eliminated the work is reduced to near zero.'

My mind went immediately to the occasion portrayed in
Acts chapter 6. Right at the start of the life of the early
church a problem reared its head which threatened the well-
being and harmony of the new community of believers. The
early church grew so rapidly that the Apostles soon found
that they were having to deal with some important but time-
consuming problems. The difficulty was that grumbling had
started amongst the believers which was threatening to affect
the whole body. At heart the problem was a good one –
church growth – but it threatened to cause division. An
increasing number of people were being added to the church
who were not 'Jerusalem' Jews, that is, Hebrew speaking and
brought up in the Hebraic tradition. The newcomers were
'Grecian' Jews – Jews of the Dispersion, who lived in different cities around the Mediterranean. Greek, not Hebrew,
was their daily tongue. This group felt that they were being
discriminated against and started to complain. It appeared
to be a justifiable complaint – the widows of the Hebrew
speaking Jews were receiving a distribution of food while the
others felt they were being neglected. This was a test case for
the Apostles. Whereas previously they had been able to over-
see each situation, now they had to prioritize their responsi-
bilities. They were, however, in no doubt where their
ultimate responsibility actually lay. They made it very plain
that although the welfare need was real and pressing it was
not something that should divert them from their first
priority of ministering the word of God. They knew that
although physical food was important there was an even

more essential constituent part of the spiritual diet without which the company of believers could not survive.

So we read:

> *'In those days when the number of disciples was increasing, the Grecian Jews among them complained against the Hebraic Jews because their widows were being overlooked in the daily distribution of food. So the Twelve gathered all the disciples together and said, "It would not be right for us to neglect the ministry of the word of God in order to wait on tables. Brothers, choose seven men from among you who are known to be full of the Spirit and wisdom. We will turn this responsibility over to them and will give our attention to prayer and the ministry of the word."*
>
> *This proposal pleased the whole group. They chose Stephen, a man full of faith and of the Holy Spirit; also Philip, Procorus, Nicanor, Timon, Parmenas, and Nicolas from Antioch, a convert to Judaism. They presented these men to the apostles, who prayed and laid their hands on them.*
>
> *So the word of God spread. The number of disciples in Jerusalem increased rapidly, and a large number of priests became obedient to the faith.'* (Acts 6:1–7)

The early church had discovered something that we need to re-discover, namely, that the church is not here just to fulfil a social programme, however worthy and necessary that may be. The Hebrew and Greek widows needed food and they got food. They did not get their food, however, at the expense of the word of God. In the church today, especially in these times of such liberal influence, there has been a divide between what is called the 'social' gospel and the 'evangelistic' gospel. As far as the preachers and teachers of the New Testament were concerned that would not have been viewed as a legitimate distinction. It is very clear that the New Testament encourages us to take care of the poor, the needy, the fatherless and the widow. However, neither those who were needy nor the needs of people, ever deflected the early Apostles from their first love, which was the declaration of the word of God. As an old professor of mine never tired of reminding us, it is not a question of either/or but both/and.

Four Principles

A closer look at this Scripture will show us four important steps which were taken by the leaders of the early Christian community. They give us some insight to their concern and the importance they attached to the continued revelation of the living word of God within the body of believers.

Firstly, they established the principle

It would not be right, they insisted, for them to neglect the ministry of the word of God in order to wait on tables (Acts 6:2). In no way, the Apostles said, will anything ever be so worthy or urgent as to distract us from what we feel is absolutely important. Here surely is a principle which needs to be re-affirmed among the people of God today. As a preacher myself, I know there are many things that clamour for our involvement. Whenever we make a determined effort to apply ourselves to receiving and preparing the word it seems that we are suddenly surrounded by so many other seemingly legitimate demands. People demanding answers, demanding action, demanding involvement. These are practical necessities, but the Bible teaches us that such necessities need to be secondary to the main call of God upon our lives. No one can declare the word of God without first hearing the word of God themselves. If we don't take time to listen to what God is saying because of all the distraction that's around we will never be in a place to proclaim the word of God to others. It wouldn't be right. It's necessary to prepare the heart for the word of God. Until this principle is established amongst us in our present situation we will never see the resurrection of the living, vital ministry of God's word.

Secondly, they made a proposal

Their proposal was simple. Choose out other men, they said, who are equipped by God in this particular situation to deal with the problem. Acts 6:5 tells us that their proposal pleased the whole group. The believers, at the behest of the Apostles, chose other men to liberate those whose calling it was to bring the word of God to the company. This was such an important action.

As I travel in my ministry I find myself constantly praying that in our churches and fellowships today we might wake up to the need for the same sort of action to be taken. I frequently come across pastors, ministers, preachers and other leaders who are suffering burn-out because the demands of people in so many other areas of life are being laid upon them. Servants who once felt so called to the ministry of the word and now are not free to fulfil their ministry because of the inordinate burdens that are laid on them.

Dr Vance Havner expressed it something like this:

> 'I think preachers are getting lost in a multitude of smaller duties. The preacher has a place in the economy of God. He is in danger of becoming so involved with secondary affairs that he loses his prophetic gift. The devil doesn't care how great a success a preacher is in any other field, if he can just kill the prophet in him.'

It is right and not wrong to feel called to the ministry of the Word of God and it is essential that those who have this calling are free to be able to fulfil it.

Perhaps those who feel called to be spiritual communicators will make a new commitment as they read this not to let any other priority establish itself above that to which they have been called. If there is the seed of a preacher in you; if there is the birthing of a teacher in you; if there is the spirit of prophecy in you – don't let anything else quench that spirit or it will destroy you. The calling to proclaim God's word has been birthed in you by God. It is an awesome thing which must be protected at all costs. The Apostles appreciated this, and so must we.

Another thing we notice from the Scripture, is that they just didn't choose anybody to wait on tables. They were men who were *'known to be full of the Spirit and wisdom'*. This is what it's going to take to release preaching again in the church today. There must be a body of people full of wisdom and the Holy Spirit to be the support ministry to those called to preach. Then preaching, teaching and the proper exercise of the prophet can stand up in its rightful place, like a jewel in its proper setting.

Thirdly, they established a priority

Acts 6:4 tells us that they made their own commitment clear: *'We ... will give our attention to prayer and the ministry of the word.'* Elsewhere it is said of Paul that he *'devoted himself exclusively'* to preaching (Acts 18:5). In many quarters today that would be regarded as a foolish thing to do. After all we live in a world pressed in by so many seemingly practical and urgent needs. To think that a man or woman should devote themselves exclusively to the proclamation of the word of God might be regarded, in some quarters, as a pointless exercise. God, however, sees it differently. He declared His mind long ago in Deuteronomy:

> *'Man does not live on bread alone but on every word that comes from the mouth of the Lord.'*
>
> (Deuteronomy 8:3)

These are the words that Jesus himself repeated during His own ministry and here right at the beginning of the church's history we see this principle being established.

Fourthly, they enjoyed the product of their actions

Acts 6:7 highlights the powerful effect of their decisions:

> *'So the word of God spread. The number of disciples in Jerusalem increased rapidly, and a large number of priests became obedient to the faith.'*

The last comment is very illuminating. I guess the priests would not have been attracted to this new Way unless the word of God had been at its centre in the power of the Holy Spirit. This, of course, is the important thing. We are not speaking here of some dead, dry, dull, didactic word with no power or personal relevance. The word, for the New Testament, equals power because it comes with all the force and vitality of the Spirit of God.

So Paul makes clear when he speaks in 2 Corinthians 3:6:

> *'He has made us competent as ministers of a new covenant – not of the letter but of the Spirit; for the letter kills, but the Spirit gives life.'*

The Apostles established their principle, they presented their proposal, they affirmed their priority, and they enjoyed the fruit of their action. The word spread and the number of disciples increased rapidly. This is, it seems to me a divine principle. In the midst of all our mechanisms and plans of action for church growth, we need to reaffirm these basic realities.

The haunting words of Amos the prophet which he proclaimed to the disobedient people of Israel may well sound in our ears:

> *'"The days are coming," declares the Sovereign Lord, "when I will send a famine through the land – not a famine of food or a thirst for water, but a famine of hearing the words of the Lord."'*　　　　　(Amos 8:11)

These words generate a feeling of dread within my spirit. What would it be like to be part of a generation that has no word from the Lord? This is the essence of preaching, it is the proclamation of God's living word in this moment. The words of Watchman Nee with which we started need to be taken so seriously:

> 'No word, no work. When the word of God is eliminated the work is reduced to near zero.'

We have been speaking a lot about the ministry of the Word. What exactly do we mean by a phrase like this? Why not just speak of preaching or teaching. Well, the answer is simple. Preaching and teaching are functional means of doing something but they themselves need to serve a deeper purpose. And that purpose is to dispense God's living word into the hearts and life situations of those to whom we speak.

This was a truth which became very real to me in the days that followed my first profound and personal encounter with the Holy Spirit. It seemed I had always been a preacher. The one sensation I am conscious of from the very early days of my Christian experience as a boy is that of a deep inner longing to preach. As the years progressed I got plenty of practice until, at last, I found myself ordained to the ministry of the Word and Sacrament. Over the years I applied myself as best I knew how and I think the results were not the worst the world or the church has ever seen. I loved the Scriptures. The various nuances of text and insight. The power of background and culture. Even the difficulties that occasionally raised their head for which there seemed no really satisfactory answer. All of these, and more, captivated my interest. However, the day the Spirit came made it all so different. It suddenly dawned on me that perhaps I had been more interested in the craft than the revelation. In fact, words like revelation would have been foreign to my idea of preaching affected as it was by my earlier ultra-conservative influences and later by more radical and liberal points of view.

It is at this point that some further insights of Watchman Nee came to my rescue. It is not that I hadn't thought these things for myself. It was just so refreshing to read someone else from a bygone generation who was thinking the same thoughts alongside one's own. I think it may be helpful to consider three insights which seem to be important.

Firstly, when we speak of the ministry of the Word we are recognising that we mean something spiritual and not just physical

To some these words may sound strange. For those of us who have lived through the sort of process I have just described they will be quite clear. What I mean is this. It is very possible to preach from the Bible, about the Bible, around the Bible without·ever expounding or declaring the word of God through the Bible! To speak of preaching being physical rather than spiritual means that we can titillate people's minds with all the interesting facts concerning the Scriptures without exposing them to the power of the living word that comes through the Scriptures. Many modern preachers have been trained to become skilled artisans in the facts and configurations of the Bible. They can delight us with details of background, culture, linguistics, history and so on without ever confronting their hearers with the life-challenging and life-changing revelation of a holy God.

As Watchman Nee puts it:

> 'There is a word in the Bible which is beyond Greek or Hebrew – it is the word which all ministers seek to know. It is the word of God.' [2]

This doesn't mean that the word is irrelevant to human practicalities. On the contrary, to say that the word is spiritual means that it is a word of power, of heart and of reality. So often we hear preachers giving people surface information from the Bible. We can all talk about the history of the Old Testament, or how the books relate to one another, giving dates and insights; we can speak about the people and the background; discuss the great saints – Abraham, Moses, Elijah – but it may still fall far short of the ministry of the word.

If we're going to be ministers of God's word, there is something here we need to grasp. We need to be looking for the depth, vitality and revelation which come from God's word. It's not just a matter of presenting people with the physical and the external – that won't change their lives. They need the spiritual, the depth. What is God saying today in the power of the Holy Spirit? That's what we need to minister. That's the word of life.

Secondly, the ministry of the Word has one chief aim in view

In the words of Watchman Nee again, 'It supplies the church with Christ.'

This is the very point that Paul makes when he writes to the believers in Colossae. He exhorts them:

> *'Let the word of Christ dwell in you richly as you teach and admonish one another with all wisdom.'*
>
> (Colossians 3:16)

The emphasis here is not so much on the idea of the word of Christ dwelling in every individual believer, although that surely is needful. Rather the thought is of a corporate indwelling. Let the word of God dwell amongst you. Here is a picture of the true church. A body of people amongst whom the word of God is present. *'Teach . . . one another'* – again our word *'didasko'*. Not a dead word, not just another sermon or lecture, but the living word, dwelling *'in you'*.

The words of the preacher are to bring the word of the ascended Christ. That's an awesome thing. To think that a human being can so speak as to transmit revelation from the throne of God! By the power of His Holy Spirit, Christ becomes dynamically present and real in the minds of men and women. As Paul said to the Corinthians:

> *'We do not preach ourselves, but Jesus Christ as Lord.'*
>
> (2 Corinthians 4:5)

What an awesome thing it is to be a preacher! It's not about ourselves; not about our style or mechanism – our calling is to bring Christ.

The very words are important. Paul does not describe it as the word of Jesus but the word of Christ. One of the main insights of the New Testament concerning the post-Pentecost church is that the work of the Spirit is the manifestation of the will and purpose of the ascended Christ pouring out His anointing among His people. It has been fashionable in some circles of biblical study to put a lot of emphasis on the Jesus of history but the revelation of the Spirit has more to do with the reality of the present Christ in our midst. The Anointed one anoints others. Here is the mystery and the wonder of it. That it is through the faithful declaration of His word in the power of the Spirit that Christ is known within the company of His people.

Thirdly, the ministry of the Word is nothing short of the presentation of the revelation of God Himself

Paul gets to grip with the real heart of preaching and teaching when he describes his own commission:

> '...the commission God gave me to present to you the word of God in its fulness – the mystery that has been kept hidden for ages and generations, but is now disclosed to the saints.'   (Colossians 1:25)

The ministry of the word should be both detailed and dynamic. It should bring into and make real within our present experience the revelation of God.

Some people react to this sort of language with fear. Whenever we speak of revelation in present tense terms they imagine that some way or another we mean to add to the revelation of the Scriptures. This isn't about adding to the Bible. This is the Holy Spirit taking all that God has already said and building a new dimension through it into our lives. Every time a preacher utters the living word, God adds another building block into the movement of His revelation.

If this was true of each word spoken out in churches today the effect would be incredible! People would either be queueing to get into church or trying to stay as far away as possible! That is the effect of the word of truth – it brings light into every situation. It brings freedom and it brings exposure. Is this happening in our churches today? Is the word that people hear so dynamic that they thirst for more of it? Or are they so convicted that they run from it? There were no nominal Christians in the early church.

Of course, this is radical talk. On the other hand the very language that we use to describe our preaching gives the lie to our attitudes. We speak of giving a sermon or a talk, or bringing the message or address. When people invite me to give an address I often feel tempted to do just that! We are called to declare the deep, underflowing revelation of God that brings life to our spirit! Jesus said:

> '...the flesh counts for nothing. The words I have spoken to you, they are spirit and they are life.'
>
> (John 6:63)

The New Testament word for minister, highlights what I am saying. The word is *'diakonos'*, from which we get our word 'deacon'. It means 'servant'. Jesus said, *'I am among you as one who serves'* (Luke 22:27). Every preacher and teacher worth their salt is a servant coming with a golden platter of the greatest food the world has ever received. We are to serve people with something that should nourish their souls in the power of the Holy Spirit. What a privilege! We are not just to bring a repetitive word, a creed that is worn out with familiarity and sometimes contempt, we are to bring the word of God, detailed and dynamic for today. We are not just to give messages, talks, homilies, sermons. The New Testament says that we are to speak as the very 'oracles' of God. Let's get a grip of this! We need a fire in our bones! It's not just passion, of course, that makes preaching – passion by itself is just hot air. But we do need to be passionate about what we believe! Someone once said that passion is the preacher's love of a lost soul at a white heat.

Richard Baxter, the great puritan preacher said:

'I'd preach as though I should ne'er preach again, as a dying man to dying men.'[3]

References

1. Nee, Watchman. 1971. *The Ministry of God's Word*. Christian Fellowship Publishers Inc.
2. Nee, Watchman. 1971. *The Ministry of God's Word*. Christian Fellowship Publishers Inc.
3. Fant, C.E. Jr, Pinson, W.E. Jr and Hammer D.E. (research associate). 1971. *Twenty Centuries of Great Preaching* (13 vol. series). Word Inc.

Chapter 4

Illumination of the Spirit

One of the most important issues in the realm of spiritual communication is the question of revelation. One dictionary definition of the word revelation runs like this:

'a fact disclosed or revealed, especially in a dramatic or surprising way.'

This sort of definition comes close to what is meant by revelation in the terms we want to consider it here. Watchman Nee, in his book *The Ministry of God's Word* uses some words which highlight both the urgency and the nature of revelation in this sense. He says that there are:

'Two different realms; one is that of doctrine, the other is that of revelation: the first can be attained with a little effort, a little cleverness and a little eloquence, the second is beyond human ability.' [1]

Now I am sure that Nee is not denying the need for some doctrinal definition. Right doctrine is important. Doctrine is an attempt to give what we perceive to be biblical truth some structure. Revelation, however, is something different from doctrine, indeed it is what should give doctrine birth. It is also beyond doctrine inasmuch as doctrine by itself can be a dead letter and a bad taskmaster. Revelation is the breath of life for the believer. Doctrine may save us from heresy but it might not lead us into life. The channel of revelation is from the Holy Spirit into the human spirit. This is how Paul perceives it when he says in Galatians 1:12:

> *'I did not receive it from any man, nor was I taught it; rather, I received it by revelation from Jesus Christ.'*

Paul was not suggesting that he had some private gospel which was different to that received by other apostles or believers. He is making the point that for it to be real and powerful it needs to come by revelation into the spirit. For Paul this is the essence of the present work of the Spirit in the experience of the believer. He has come to enable our understanding and communication of what God has done for us. Apart from this deep personal process of the Spirit within us the gospel remains at the level of a history lesson or a doctrinal formula.

> *'The Spirit searches all things, even the deep things of God. For who among men knows the thoughts of a man except the man's spirit within him? In the same way, no-one knows the thoughts of God except the Spirit of God. We have not received the spirit of the world, but the Spirit who is from God, that we may understand what God has freely given us. This is what we speak, not in words taught us by human wisdom, but in words taught by the Spirit, expressing spiritual truths in spiritual words. The man without the Spirit does not accept the things that come from the Spirit of God, for they are foolishness to him, and he cannot understand them because they are spiritually discerned. The spiritual man makes judgements about all things, but he himself is not subject to any man's judgement.*
> *"For who has known the mind of the Lord that he may instruct him?"*
> *But we have the mind of Christ.'*

(1 Corinthians 2:10–16)

1. The Essence of Revelation

Paul touches the heart of the matter in his prayer for the believers at Ephesus when he says:

> *'I keep asking that the God of our Lord Jesus Christ, the glorious Father, may give you the Spirit of wisdom and revelation, so that you may know him better. I pray also that the eyes of your heart may be enlightened in order that you may know the hope to which he has called you.'*
>
> (Ephesians 1: 17, 18)

Revelation is, first of all then, a breakthrough by the Holy Spirit

It is a movement of illumination by the Holy Spirit, it is an enlightenment of our minds and spirit. The process may have lasted over a period of time but the end of the matter is very sudden as the light breaks in. Such a breakthrough can take place in a whole number of different situations. Perhaps it comes as part of the process of studying the Scriptures. It may be that some difficult text which has not opened up before suddenly takes on a fresh meaning and we are able to see its significance in a completely new way. Or maybe we are dealing with some practical challenge where the way ahead seems so closed up and all the options closed when suddenly we receive a sense of direction and there before us lies the answer which previously seemed so elusive.

Such a movement can take place anywhere. It may happen while we are seriously studying the Scriptures or preparing to bring a word. Or it may take place as we are driving along during one of those moments of mental and spiritual reflection. Suddenly the light breaks through and what seemed dark and impervious all of a sudden becomes clear and straightforward. The old saints used to describe their initial Christian experience in this way. They said they had seen the light and perhaps they were not far from the truth. In fact, they were right on the button! It takes the action of the Holy Spirit to open our eyes to what we were previously blind to or ignorant of. In a moment He can make the most profound needs and spiritual truths clear.

So revelation is a breakthrough of the Holy Spirit to the inner man – an inner illumination of the human mind and spirit which brings with it a whole new understanding of what God says and desires.

Revelation does not only bring light, it brings a sense of the immediacy of God and with that a response from within our spirits. The response will depend on the nature of the truth which has been revealed. It could be a great sense of relief as we see the difficulty resolved or the burden lifted. On the other hand it could bring an overwhelming sense of responsibility, as it did to Isaiah, as we realise the implications of what we have seen for our lives.

2. The Process of Revelation

When writing about preaching Dr D.W. Cleverley-Ford once said that successful communication 'involves a double process of thoughts into words and words back into thoughts.' He is saying, in his own way, what I am trying to share here with regard to revelation. Watchman Nee says that there has to be 'an inner word' before there can be 'an outer word.'

Most people receive a lot of revelation but don't live in the full good of it because they don't understand the process by which it operates in their spirit. It is not simply a matter of receiving insight or good ideas from the Holy Spirit. Many believers experience breakthroughs in their spirit but within a brief period of time the significance or deeper meaning of it has been lost. This is especially the case with revelation which we want to share with or pass on to other people. Most of us know the feeling of having seen something in a very fresh and powerful way only to discover a few days later when we try and share it with others that the essence and power of the revelation seem to have departed. That is the sort of thing which happens when we don't take time to reflect on the processes of revelation. To understand the steps will help us to retain the good of what we see and hear and will certainly put us in a much better situation when it comes to sharing it with other people.

At this point I want to acknowledge my indebtedness to the insights of Watchman Nee in his book to which I have already alluded several times. It is not my intention merely to regurgitate what someone else has written but I found my own spirit so stimulated with his insights at this particular point that I have no hesitation in following his thoughts.

In a nutshell what he says is that **there are three important stages in the process of revelation**. These three processes can be described simply as:
– **receiving the light,**
– **fixing the light,** and
– **sharing the light.**
Nee expresses it like this:

> 'Light first shines into the spirit, but God does not purpose to have the light remain there. He wishes the light to reach the understanding. After light has reached the understanding, it no longer passes away but can be fixed. Revelation is not permanent in nature; it is like lightning which flashes and passes away. But when light shines and man's understanding takes it in and knows its meaning, then the light is fixed and we know its content. When the light is only in the spirit it comes and goes freely, but once it enters our thought and understanding it becomes anchored. From then on we are able to use the light.'[2]

I am sure that we all can identify with what Nee means when he says that revelation is like lightning which flashes and is gone. How many times we have received something in our spirit but because the due processes of revelation have not been followed through we are, in the end, left with a good impression and perhaps a feeling of well-being or challenge but nothing very substantial on which to base later action or communications.

Personally Speaking

A quick review of the steps involved in the process of revelation will help us to grasp more clearly what is required. I would say that if we are to recapture anything of what the New Testament sees as prophetic preaching and teaching these principles are urgently important. They may be significant for every Christian believer but, if that is so, then they are even more significant in the experience of any person who feels called to the ministry of the word of God in the body of Christ today.

(a) Receiving the light

We have already established that the essence of revelation is a breakthrough of light. This is consistent with the character of God and with the declarations of Jesus Himself as the light of the world. The New Testament many times contrasts the light with the darkness and sees the change that comes with Christian confession as a direct transfer from the realm of darkness into the realm of light in the kingdom of God (Ephesians 5:8 for example).

Some, of course, may protest that such a view contradicts the principles of human reason. I don't think so, it simply puts reason in its rightful place. The overriding sin of the Enlightenment is to put reason above revelation. Reason is not unimportant but in the right place it is the servant of revelation and not its master. With reason in charge man is in control but when we are dependent on the breakthrough of the Holy Spirit then we are at the mercy of God.

(b) Fixing the light

David the psalmist said,

> *'I have hidden your word in my heart that I might not sin against you.'*　　　　　　　　　　(Psalm 119:11)

The word of God was something that was fixed within him. It was not about to fade away but was established in his mind and spirit so that he could meditate on it and follow through its meaning for his daily life.

The challenge of receiving, retaining and building on the revelation we receive is, I believe, one of the greatest challenges to Christian experience today. As we have already seen it is the nature of light to be transient and fleeting. The images and ideas which it throws up can be equally passing unless we learn the disciplines of taking hold of the word, establishing it within our minds and hearts and then learning to build on it in such a way that it becomes the foundation either for action or communication.

I suppose a simple illustration might be taken from the realm of photography. When a film has been developed it needs to be passed through some sort of fixing fluid if it is to remain as a print on the paper. Unless it is fixed it will fade within a short time and all the efforts of the photographer will have been in vain. It is like this with revelation. The Holy Spirit breaks through with the light of spiritual illumination, but unless we take steps to fix the light the image of the word will disappear, and we will be left without the good of the revelation of God.

This is why, somewhere else, Nee says that 'it takes a rich and strong mind to fix the light.' He is not suggesting that we all need to be intellectuals to receive revelation from God. He is, however, making a point that is very valid for our own time. Unless we have disciplined our minds to some degree and have exposed our thoughts and emotions to the impact and discipline of the Scriptures we might find that we are unable to retain divine truth no matter how often it is given. One of the biggest problems of Christian living today is what can only be described as 'scatty-mindedness'. Perhaps it is because in life as a whole we are exposed to so many rapidly changes images and scenarios. Through the medium of television for example our eyes and minds receive literally thousands of images within the space of one programme. This is meant to keep our attention and communicate to us through speed and repetition. Of course, in its own way it does that but at the same time it has the effect of dulling our mental capacity for concentration and creativity. Most of the thinking, if there is any, is done for us and we become slaves of the ever-changing scene in which drama and hype rule the roost.

The net result is that we become people who receive information in such a way, that it makes a brief and shallow impact on us to the degree that in our generation there are those who cannot tell the difference between real events and the dramatic action of the latest police thriller. It seems that unless emotional impulses follow one after the other in quick succession people's inner imagination goes dead.

It is for this reason that the New Testament sometimes speaks of the mind in the way it does. In Romans chapter 12 Paul reminds us of the need to have our minds renewed in the power of God so that we will not be squeezed into the mould of the world around us. Nowhere is this more important than in the realm of spiritual revelation. It may seem that all our talk about the breakthrough of light bears the same hallmarks as the impulses of modern communication. There is a great difference, however, in that God does not send us these experiences of revelation to titillate our imagination or for our amusement. They are meant to lead us deeper into an understanding and appreciation of that which God has to say to or through us. For this reason, they cannot only be transient but need to be fixed and established in our hearts and minds so that we can let the word develop in us.

This is why I recommend that Christians live in the Scriptures as well as in the exercises of their spirit through prayer and meditation on the things of God. To this end I warmly commend a book written by a dear friend of mine Campbell McAlpine. It is the best help available to those who want to learn how to establish God's word in their heart and is called *The Practice of Biblical Meditation*.[3] Campbell shows us how to prepare to listen to God and how to let the word of God be established in our minds and hearts through meditation on the Scriptures.

The point about this is simple. Unless there is already a bedding of godly material in our minds and spirits it will be much more difficult to retain the light once it comes to us. It really helps a great deal if there is a scattering, so to speak, of empathetic material within us to which the new light can attach. The word within us can then be gathered round the fresh light and so substantiate it within us. This is the process of building up or establishing the word, or, as it has been described already, of fixing the light. So a word can be formed in the heart and mind which becomes something that can be considered and meditated upon, it can grow and be enlarged. If necessary, it can be refined; it can certainly be tested.

This last point is so important because it seems that so many people lack the power of discernment. They don't seem to have the capacity to say whether a word has come from God or some other source. They don't seem able to discriminate between their own vivid imagination and the revelation work of the Holy Spirit. Now we must not be too surprised at this because the Holy Spirit engages every one of our faculties when He begins to work within us. Sometimes our intellects will be more to the fore; at other times it will be our feelings which will grasp the word first. Or it may be that the first movement of revelation comes by means of a vision or a dream or in some such way. How then can we tell whether this is from God or not?

I would contend that the man or woman who makes it their practice to live within the Scriptures and who allows their mind to be disciplined by the written word of God will have far less trouble in such matters of discernment than the person whose mind is allowed to be dominated by all sorts of others things and so perhaps lacks the discipline of the Holy Spirit. It doesn't take a great intellect to receive and discern the inner word from God but it does take a heart and mind that knows something of the discipline of the Spirit to know what to do with revelation when it comes. The writer to the Hebrews makes the same point when he speaks of spiritual maturity:

> 'Solid food is for the mature, **who by constant use have trained themselves to distinguish good from evil.**'
> (Hebrews 5:14, emphasis added)

(c)   Sharing the light

In his discourse on the subject of spiritual revelation in 1 Corinthians chapter 2 Paul expresses the purpose of the work of the Spirit. It is to enable our understanding of what God has freely given us so that we might be able to communicate it to others.

> *'This is what we speak, not in words taught us by human wisdom but in words taught by the Spirit, expressing spiritual truths in spiritual words.'*   (1 Corinthians 2:13)

We have already established that there can be no outer word until there is a word established within our minds and hearts. A great failing of some communicators is that they only share out of their emotions. Feelings are important for effective communication but emotion needs to be the servant of understanding and not the other way round. This is particularly important for Christian communication. By its very nature our subject contains a high level of the emotional; it affects the deepest reaches of our personality and ought to affect our listeners in a similar way. Some people, in the light of this, have almost rejected any idea of proper preparation in favour of 'Spirit led' spontaneity. The result of this so-called spontaneity is often needless repetition and a poverty of any worthy thoughts or ideas which stimulate or build up the hearers.

On the other hand we are called to be witnesses to a living revelation. The word needs to be incarnated. As preachers, teachers, prophets and the like we have been chosen to bear this living word to our own generation through the channel of our hearts and minds which have been prepared in the power of the Holy Spirit. Paul says that it is to be expressed through 'spiritual words'. I always have a bit of fun when I am speaking about this with a live audience in a seminar. I ask them to give some examples of spiritual words. The results are always interesting! Out come words like 'justification', 'redemption', 'holiness', 'faith', 'sanctification' and the like. But these are not spiritual words. They are no more spiritual than any other words we might use to express what we believe. Now before you protest consider this. Words like those I have just exampled are technical terms which we use to package our thoughts and ideas concerning the gospel and our Christian life and belief. To an outsider words like these would be almost meaningless. No, when he speaks of expressing spiritual truths in spiritual words Paul does not mean the technical jargon of Christian faith. He means that we speak in words which carry with them the direct power of the Holy Spirit! To put it another way, our words are like the cable which carries electric power. No cable, no power where you want it. But you could have cable without power!

The pressure of the word

Watchman Nee goes a step further in his explanation of this process. He highlights something that every spiritual communicator knows to be a fact. That revelation of the sort we have been considering carries with it another important effect. It brings about an inward pressure in the spirit of the person to whom God gives the revelation. I have found this to be true in every instance when I have known God speak to me. The pressure may be that of the joy of seeing something for the first time. We tend not to be able to contain such experiences of revelation inside ourselves for too long. Of course, we need to be careful with whom we share what we have been shown by God. It may be that what we have received is of a personal nature and is not meant for widespread consumption. In that case we may share it with only a chosen few or, indeed, with only one person. If we do otherwise there will be a danger that the word will be spoiled and the power and significance of it will be severely diminished.

For the person called to public communication, however, the case is different. This pressure is the motivational element which the Spirit brings. It gives a sense of worth, urgency, weight and excitement to the word of God within. Perhaps this is what the Old Testament prophets meant when they spoke of the burden of the Lord. Nee puts it this way:

> 'The supply of the word is the supply of the Spirit. When the Spirit is released, power, light, life, the Holy Spirit and pressure are all released.'[4]

When we speak it is meant to bring about a discharge of this burden, this pressure from the Lord. The discharge of this pressure is also what brings an effect about in the lives of those who listen. I believe that other people sense when a speaker is in the process of discharging a burden and that, as a result, they receive the word in their own spirits at a different level.

3. The Flow of the Spirit

From both Scripture and experience we can identify a number of elements in the operation of the Holy Spirit in His ministry of revelation. This flow of the Spirit is what brings revelation to completion within our experience so that the word that is birthed within produces a living word that becomes effective through us and finds a lodging place in the experience of others.

(a) Inspiration

It is no accident that one of the most powerful images associated with the work of the Spirit in Scripture is that of the wind. Neither is it accidental that when Jesus imparted the Spirit to His disciples it is recorded that He breathed on them. Paul reminds us that the same reality of inspiration is at the heart of the Spirit's work in bringing the Scriptures to birth.

> *'All scripture is God-breathed and is useful for teaching, rebuking, correcting and training in righteousness.'*
>
> (2 Timothy 3:16)

The primary work of the Spirit, therefore, lies within the hearts and minds of those who first produced the Scriptures. Inspiration does not stop here, however. For the word to be effective in a living way in every generation there needs to be an ongoing work of inspiration. The promise of Jesus and the Scriptures is that this principle of inspiration is the power that will lie at the heart of all effective ministry in the Spirit. We don't only need the letter of the word in us, we need the vitality of the Spirit in us. As Paul says:

> *'He has made us competent as ministers of a new cove-nant – not of the letter but of the Spirit, for the letter kills but the Spirit gives life.'*   (2 Corinthians 3:6)

(b) Understanding

Paul says in his letter to the Corinthians that:

> *'We have not received the spirit of the world, but the Spirit who is from God, that we may understand what God has freely given us.'*   (1 Corinthians 2:12)

One of the outstanding incidents in the experience of the early church was that of Philip the evangelist who was carried by the Holy Spirit to witness to the Ethiopian eunuch. At that moment the eunuch was reading from the prophecy of Isaiah. Philip asked the man whether or not he understood what he was reading. His answer is illuminating:

> *'"How can I," he said, "unless someone explains it to me?"'*   (Acts 8:31)

The Spirit is given, says Paul, so that we might understand the things that God has freely given us (1 Corinthians 2:12). This is not the place to start a long discussion on the difficulties of interpretation with regard to the Scriptures. Generally, I am in agreement with the sort of statement made by Kevin Connor in his book *Foundations of Christian Doctrine* when he says:

'Generally speaking, Bible believing Christians are united in accepting the facts of revelation and inspiration. However, the major divisions concern interpretation and application.'[5]

I am in no doubt at all, however, that those who come to the Scriptures with an open heart, relying on the help of the Holy Spirit will develop measures of spiritual understanding far beyond their human abilities and their natural capacities. It is the same with the operations of the Spirit in areas of revelation beyond the biblical text, when we are led through the inner voice or through words or dreams. It takes the Spirit to interpret all these things to our minds so that we might be able to follow the implications of God's word in our life's ministries.

(c) Operation

'For prophecy never had its origin in the will of man, but men spoke from God as they were carried along by the Holy Spirit.' (2 Peter 1:21)

The Spirit of God does not only open up our understanding, it is He who enables our communication. This movement of the Spirit is what lies at the heart of every authentic sharing of the word of God. He gives a spirit of freedom, a spirit of liberty. Our motivation for speaking comes from the Holy Spirit. Our education on the subject comes from the Spirit. The discipline in our will comes from the Spirit. The Spirit is the one who operates in us as we prepare to share the words which God has given us.

(d) Communication

We have already seen what Paul means when he says,

'This is what we speak, not in words taught us by human wisdom but in words taught by the Spirit, expressing spiritual truths in spiritual words.' (1 Corinthians 2:13)

He does not mean that we have to speak in some religious mumbo-jumbo. He means that when we speak what God gives us to share our words are meant to convey the power of the Holy Spirit. They are the conduit by which spiritual power is released into the inner being of all who listen in faith. We can recall the words of Tom Allen about Billy Graham which were quoted right at the start of this book. When people were asked about his message Allen summed up their response; 'the verdict is this: we understand what this man is saying.'

It would no doubt be an affront to some preachers to suggest that plain people did not understand the framework of their language but sadly this is the case. The Holy Spirit has not come to make us verbal technicians in theological jargon but to release through us a life-giving word from God Himself.

(e) Application

> *'The word of God is living and active. Sharper than any two-edged sword.'*   (Hebrews 4:12)

The word penetrates the inner heart and it is part of our communication of the word to know how it should be applied to people's needs. How do we bring the word of God to bear in people's lives so that it does what He intends it to do? Do we need to do anything but declare it or preach it? I will deal elsewhere with when and how we should minister after the declaration of the word. Let me just say at this point that we need to be as dependent on the revelation of the Holy Spirit here as anywhere else in the whole process. I have seen the word ruined and robbed from people because someone insisted on doing something else after they had spoken the word. Equally, I have been aware on other occasions of the need of some form of ministry to enable people to receive the implications of the word into the depths of their hearts and lives. It is after all, the unique work of the Spirit of God Himself to apply the word and bring out its consequences in human experience. Even at this point we are only followers after divine activity.

4. The Effect of Revelation

There are so many points to be made here. Let me underline **four important and vital effects** which flow from revelation. I believe these are so essential in the situation we face in the body of Christ today.

(a) Encouragement

Paul describes the result of the living word from God being present in the fellowship of God's people when he says in 1 Corinthians 14:3,

> *'everyone who prophesies speaks to men for their strengthening, encouragement and comfort.'*

Revelation may bring conviction. It may bring warning and correction. But at heart the purpose of the Father is to build up the people of Christ. Even a word of warning or correction correctly heeded will result in a new experience of forgiveness and encouragement. This needs to be our aim in all our spiritual communications, to build up, strengthen and encourage our fellow believers. The word rightly shared brings a new strength of purpose and a fresh confidence to the heart in a way that only God's word can.

(b) Conviction

In 1 Corinthians 14:24 Paul teaches another important lesson. He says,

> *'if an unbeliever or someone who does not understand comes in while everybody is prophesying, he will be convinced . . . that he is a sinner.'*

This is the operation of the Holy Spirit. Jesus said that

when the Spirit came He would convince the world of sin and of righteousness and of judgement. The person who hears this revelation in the midst of the people of God, will fall down with an open heart and say 'God is here!'

(c) Inspiration

Again in 1 Corinthians 14 Paul challenges the sort of exercise which purports to be an expression of God's word but is actually nothing but a manifestation of the flesh. In the middle of his argument Paul highlights this important principle in verse 8,

> 'if the trumpet does not sound a clear call, who will get ready for battle?'

True declaration of the word of God, which is the result of revelation, should stimulate and inspire. It should sound a certain trumpet note in the hearts and minds of those who listen in faith and motivate them to follow the direction of the word.

(d) Guidance

In Acts 11:27 we have an instance which demonstrates just how powerful the sharing of a word of revelation can be in the experience of a fellowship of God's people.

> 'During this time some prophets came down from Jerusalem to Antioch. One of them named Agabus, stood up and through the Spirit predicted that a severe famine would spread over the entire Roman world. The disciples ... decided to provide help ... this they did, sending their gift ... by Barnabas and Saul.'

When God's word comes like this it shows us what to do. Through the word of God received personally, received through a preacher or received through a prophet like Agabus, people know what God intends. It is the essence of spiritual communication that it should increase our awareness of and openness to what the will of God is in every situation.

Revelation brings a cutting edge. To some this might seem too aggressive, but I think it is a true biblical image of the operation of God's word. No true spiritual communicator wants to deal with a blunt instrument. The word of God is sharp and quick, it is alive and powerful. It is, according to Hebrews 4:12, sharper than any two-edged sword. That's sharp! What does a sharp instrument do? A sharp instrument is clinically effective. What does a blunt instrument do? A blunt instrument batters people to death. How many of us have been battered and bludgeoned to death with words? The word of revelation brings sharpness; not the kind of cutting that will kill, rather the kind of cutting that brings life.

The point is this. These four effects are realities which are so much needed amongst God's people. We need those who are prepared to declare God's word with these ends in view because they are part of God's great purpose for our human experience as He reveals His word into our lives.

References

1. Nee, Watchman. 1971. *The Ministry of God's Word.* Christian Fellowship Publishers Inc.
2. *Ibid*
3. McAlpine, Campbell. 1981. *The Practice of Biblical Meditation.* Marshall Pickering
4. Nee, Watchman. 1971. *The Ministry of God's Word.* Christian Fellowship Publishers Inc.
5. Connor, Kevin. 1980. *Foundations of Christian Doctrine.* Sovereign World

Chapter 5

Getting the Message Across

'If the trumpet does not sound a clear call, who will get ready for battle?'   (1 Corinthians 14:8)

When Paul speaks to the believers in Corinth about their use of the spiritual gifts he reminds them of the need for clarity and intelligibility in their communication. It is not a far step from his subject to ours and we can easily see how applicable to our theme the principles are that he underlines to the Corinthians. In particular this is what he says:

'Unless you speak intelligible words with your tongue, how will anyone know what you are saying? You will just be speaking into the air. Undoubtedly there are all sorts of languages in the world, yet none of them is without meaning. If then I do not grasp the meaning of what someone is saying, I am a foreigner to the speaker and he is a foreigner to me.'   (1 Corinthians 14:9–11)

It is obvious that he is speaking about something which is absolutely central to our subject of spiritual communication; simply that if whoever we are trying to communicate with doesn't understand or cannot grasp what we're saying, for whatever reason, then we might as well be speaking in a foreign language for all the good it's going to do. Proverbs 18:21 reminds us of the power of human speech when it says that the tongue has the power of life and death. It is vital for any communicator to remember this fact and take whatever steps are needed to remove any hindrance or blockage to the clear communication of the message.

I was greatly helped by the simple diagram below which was developed by Donald Ely an American teacher, to show the process of communication. It is extremely effective in its simplicity. It helps us to identify some of the practical factors that we need to consider as we approach the task.

Fields of Experience

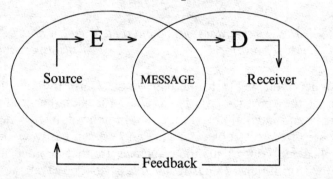

The oval on the left represents the speaker while the one on the right represents the one who is meant to be receiving the message. The caption 'Fields of Experience' written above the ovals tells us what these two ovals represent. This diagram holds good for any communicative situation between two people but is just as applicable to the communicator with a larger audience. When any one of us tries to communicate, we don't just do it in terms of words or ideas, we speak out of a field of experience and we speak into another field of experience. This colours how and what we pass on. The field of experience defines the boundary lines of one's life, experience and understanding. There are experiences within these lines which have deep emotions in them, which hold deep memories. Whilst my field of experience may be extensive it also has limitations to it. The same is true of the field of experience of any person or persons I may be speaking to.

The Place of the Message

In any real communication there needs to be an area where these two fields overlap – this is the place of the message. Unless this is the case no really dynamic communication takes place. Certainly words will pass over but there will be no meaningful interrelation and the words will not communicate to the degree that they would if these two fields of experience engage with one another.

One reason for failure in this regard lies in the fact that we forget we need to say things that have some degree of familiarity for our hearer. Even if the subject is unfamiliar, the language should be such that it will bring the subject towards the receiver. This is a great challenge for Christian preachers and teachers, especially in evangelism or subjects that people may not be familiar with if they have no biblical background.

It is, of course, quite legitimate to speak about subjects that people don't know much about, otherwise no-one would ever learn anything new! However, when we do speak of things that are unfamiliar to our audience we need to ensure that expressions, forms of address and personal involvement within the message are used in such a way as to bring the unknown element nearer to them. I'm speaking of movement here because communication isn't just verbalisation, it's an occurrence. Where the field of the speaker overlaps with that of the hearer an event should take place. Any preacher worth his salt knows this. He doesn't preach just because he feels good about it; there's a connection that has to be made and it is this connection that brings the power to the message.

Encoding and Decoding

It will be seen that the letters 'E' and 'D' are used within the two ovals to identify these two sides to any effective communication. 'E' simply stands for Encoding and 'D' for Decoding. These two letters serve as a powerful reminder of what stands at the heart of effective communication. It involves two movements within two different parties. The first involves the speaker encapsulating his or her ideas and thoughts in terms that the present audience can understand and appreciate. The second simply reminds us of the necessity for our audience to be able to receive what we say in terms they understand.

We have all had perhaps, the sort of experience when for example, we have listened to someone preaching and wondered why we are not receiving their message. The preaching may be with passion. The preacher may be obviously very involved in what he is saying and yet ... those listening don't know what he's talking about! This is the challenge of communication. We have the responsibility of making clear what God has given us in our spirit to pass to someone else. A story is told of the young curate who was preaching before his bishop. When he'd finished he came to the bishop and asked him, 'Well, how was that?' The bishop replied, ' The trouble young man, is that you spent half an hour trying to get it out of your head, instead of into mine.' The young man had not clarified his line of communication, so all the bishop was receiving was noise, with no real message.

Let's look at this question from two angles:

The Receivers

We need to consider certain factors in relation to our audience which will facilitate a clearer reception of what we are trying to communicate to them. Consider the following:

(a) Their ability to understand

If we use words, concepts or expressions that are beyond our hearers' current knowledge or capacity we will never get the message over.

This may seem too simple, but it is utterly important that we take into consideration the ability of people to understand what we're saying. Remember what Tom Allan the famous Glasgow preacher said about Billy Graham the evangelist:

> 'never mind the style or how lacking in eloquence it may be, the verdict is "we understand what this man is saying."'

How sad it is that once a person becomes a Christian, living in a totally new context and lifestyle, they seem to forget so readily where they came from and so quickly lose sight of the size of the gap between the believing and unbelieving world. A tendency soon develops to start speaking about ideas which are totally outside the frame of reference of the unbeliever and in terminology that is totally foreign to them.

(b) Their need to understand

Jesus always spoke into people's lives at their point of need. He seemed to have the ability to connect with people right where they were. For example, when He came to the woman at Sychar's well, He approached her from the point of view of His need of water and through that simple physical reality entered right inside her field of experience. He said,

> *'If you knew ... who it is that asks you for a drink, you would have asked him and he would have given you living water ... welling up to eternal life.'*   (John 4:10, 14)

Then, as another example of inter-personal communication, He used deep personal insight to see into her situation when He said *'Go, call your husband'* (John 4:16).

The effect of this was so great that, not only did she believe, but her whole village believed as well.

It is the responsibility of the communicator to create desire in his audience. If we believe, as preachers or teachers that we have something worth talking about, something that the people before us may not have heard before, then we have the responsibility to create a need for them to understand.

When the woman came to the well, she did not come expecting to meet her Messiah, or that someone would challenge her about the six men she had lived with, or that she would find a new gift of life. She met with Jesus, however, and He uncovered a need in her; a need that was there, but that she hadn't perhaps recognised. That's what a real communicator does through the power of the Spirit of God – awakens people's sense of need and quickens in them a desire to understand what's being said.

(c) The desire to understand

A whole number of different factors can, and do, affect other people's desire to hear what we're saying – their emotional equilibrium, their prejudice grid, their pre-conceived ideas, the circumstances of their life.

We need to ask the Holy Spirit for help to enable us to be sensitive to how people are or to what may be going on in their lives at the moment. Our urgency to speak with them can be misplaced if their circumstance or emotions find them in a completely different position from that which makes them open to receive our message. It may be that someone is feeling really pleased with themselves over something they have achieved. This may be totally the wrong moment to try and bring them some solemn word of warning or admonition. This is where the sensitivity of the Spirit of God is so important to the Christian communicator. It enables us to look at a person and, without even speaking to them personally, gain some inner perception of what is going on in their life. Then we can know if it's the right time to speak, the right season, or maybe at that moment a waste of time!

This is an area where inexperience or immaturity tends to rush forward too fast sometimes. Sometimes we feel the urgency of the message or the call to preach the gospel and we feel we must do it whatever the circumstances. Only later do we discover that our best endeavours of preparation and communication have fallen on deaf, albeit sometimes polite, ears simply because we ourselves have been deaf to the signals being emitted from the psyche or circumstances of the receptor audience.

With a little practice and experience we become seasoned in the word of God and know better how to operate with the things of the Spirit. We begin to know how and when to switch on our spiritual radar scanners. A word on paper has got a certain shape, but that shape can be expanded, contracted, the emphasis altered, according to what I read about the person in the Spirit. If we don't do this, then we're not really communicating. Instead it turns out to be a one-sided exercise.

(d) The conditions to receive

If you want to have a confidential, pastoral chat with someone, it's no use choosing a noisy public place to talk to them.

In other words, we need to ask whether the conditions are suitable to enable people to receive what we are saying. One of the things that I have had to learn over the years is how to master a situation, instead of letting the situation master me. There are many factors which can seriously unsettle today's Christian communicator. In earlier days some of us were brought up to sit for two hours or more through a service, never to sneeze, nudge or blink. One could just about get away with slipping a mint in one's mouth in a surreptitious moment! Now I'm not saying all of that was ideal, but there was a definite up side – we learned how to concentrate. The mobility of modern life has actually robbed people of that ability to concentrate. Another dictum was that other people mattered as much as we did, so we were careful in a meeting not to disturb other people's thoughts. Today's philosophy seems rather different with far less care about the effect of our actions in unsettling other people around us. Consequently, people are up and down in their seats, they appear to do what they fancy, take the kids to the toilet and trip in and out according to the latest whim that grabs them, without any thought about the effect on other people.

Any public communicator needs to be alert to this. If a serious point is to be made, for example, and there's a lot of activity going on there's no point in ploughing on regardless – you'll lose the point. If the point is to be made effectively then sensitivity to the situation is necessary all the time. It may even prove necessary to carry out some diversionary exercise while the disruption continues to give space for the situation to be overcome. If God gave the word, He will also find ways of getting that word across, as long as we have the common sense and spiritual sensitivity to be aware of it.

I am sure that most readers will have found themselves in situations where the speaker insisted on carrying on regardless. I was once involved in an extreme example of this at a meeting in an old Congregational church in Yorkshire. It was a building that reflected another age and the man who got up to preach was in much the same state as the building and rather nervous with it. However, he was the type of speaker that once started there was no stopping; he was going to go from the beginning to the end of what he had to say no matter what. From where I was sitting in the second row of pews, I noticed that a man in front of me had taken some sort of fit and (as far as I remember) actually subsequently died. Did this stop our preacher? No way! He just carried doggedly on! Needless to say I remember the occasion very well but I can't recall one word of what the preacher was trying to say.

The same is true with regard to very simple things. Take, for example, the question of temperature in the room or hall. Is it too hot, or too cold? Or is there a draft coming in? A real communicator is going to take factors like these into account and, if necessary, find ways around them.

The Source

We need to turn our attention next to the other end of the equation. In other words the person who is trying to communicate with the audience. Here again there are some fundamental factors to be taken into consideration.

(a) Meaning

In 1 Corinthians 14, Paul says that we are to use intelligible words so that what we communicate is meaningful to other people. There comes a point at which too many words can fudge the meaning of the message. One crime that many preachers commit is to use a great amount of redundant language. Of course, we must use certain words and repeat them for emphasis where necessary, but if we were really brutal with ourselves we would admit that many of our words are just space-fillers. Instead of clarifying the meaning, they can often have the opposite effect and leave the audience submerged under a flood of words. Clarity is of the essence.

(b) Relevance

Look at these two parallel vertical lines drawn below.

The space between the two lines is the common ground that two people may have between each other in their communication or a speaker may have with the audience. It represents an area of commonality of experience or understanding or empathy. Outside of these two lines we move into territory that is not common to the two parties. Inside the lines is **the area of relevance**. If we speak about something that falls inside the lines we are on good ground for communication. Just outside the lines on both sides is a small area that can be called the **zone of toleration**. In other words, it may be that although we are not directly speaking inside our listener's area of relevance we are, nevertheless, in close enough proximity to it to be able still to communicate effectively. The farther the speaker goes outside the area of relevance and certainly if they speak beyond the zone of toleration, the less chance there is of meaningful communication with that audience. An area of up to about ten per cent outside the line is probably the maximum limit of toleration. Outside this the audience switches off because communication is no longer taking place within or near to their area of relevance.

This is a real challenge to the Christian communicator who may be attempting to communicate new ideas to believers or, more particularly, in the attempt to share the gospel with unbelievers. The likelihood is that we will not be speaking within this zone of toleration, so then we must endeavour to bring what we are saying towards the zone of toleration of our hearers. In other words to apply the truth and to make it relevant. Not only do our words need to have meaning, they must also be seen and felt to be relevant. So then, whether it's a completely new subject, or perhaps something more technical or theological, the person listening can see how it might relate to his or her own life. Without this we might as well be talking into thin air. Mind you this is exactly what I was taught to do at the particular theological college I trained at. We were taught to look at the congregation, take a point about a metre above the heads of those in the back row and address that point on the assumption that everyone would then fall under the gaze of the speaker. It doesn't work!

(c) Presentation

We don't just listen with our ears, we listen in our minds. What's the difference? Well, the mind isn't impacted only by sounds, but also visually. If the subject can be presented in such a way that people can see clear points of progression with their minds then what is said will have a much bigger impact. Each point that is made in communication should be a memory aid; something to help and stimulate the memory.

(d) Sensitivity

We need to remain open at all times to the responses of our hearers. When we preach effectively we can see the word of God taking root and doing something in people's lives. Preaching may seem to be a monologue but in this sense it is also a dialogue. The Christian communicator must rely on the Spirit's help to sense the responses of the audience. In this way they are having an unspoken conversation with the audience.

The Nature of Communication

We have already seen that spiritual communication is not just about words. Communication is not just verbal, words need to be empowered. Of course, as believers, we know that this power comes from the Holy Spirit, but there's also the human factor to take into consideration. E.M. Bounds was a chaplain during the American Civil War. He was a man of great spiritual insight and prayer who had the gift of putting profound truth in a simple nutshell. He once said that: 'God anoints men, not machines.' Machines are probably one of the greatest menaces in our modern society as far as meaningful personal communication is concerned. Certainly the threat is profoundly greater than it ever was to E.M. Bounds. I don't believe that the computer could ever take the place of the preacher, nor will the fax supplant the person however useful they prove to be in other areas. Although books are good, they can never take the place of a real live preacher. Why? Because God incarnates His truth within the experience and gift of human vessels. The empowering of the words comes through the gifting of the personality.

Today they even make cars that can speak to you. They will tell you if lights have been left on. It is communication of a sort, and valuable, but it has no flow of personality in it – it's metallic and mechanical. There's a lot of communication around like that. When I prepare to fly I often need to telephone for a weather report and I have to pinch myself sometimes to remember that what I am listening to is not a real person but a computer generated voice. The information comes through but any interplay between human personalities is completely absent. Where it is a matter of facts this may not be so important but when it comes to preaching or teaching or other forms of spiritual communication God anoints men and women and what we are and what we do empowers the words.

Non-Verbal Communication

'I would believe in their salvation, if they looked a little bit more like they were saved.'

So said Friedrich Nietzsche an atheist philosopher of the last century who was totally anti-Christian. Yet he wasn't satisfied with life around him. He talked about looking and waiting for a type of people who would be 'the stronger ones, more triumphant ones ... built squarely in body and soul.' He couldn't see any evidence of that in Christians. There are many preachers that sadly may buffer his sort of viewpoint – 'If only I could see some life in them, I would believe them a bit more.' Their words are alright, their structure wonderful, but they have no power. Why? Because the words are not empowered by the person.

I once heard it said that non-verbal communication is sixteen times more powerful than verbal communication.

I am not sure how this can be measured so accurately. However, I can understand the claim. For example, if you tell someone you love them, what you say with your eyes and with your touch is far more convincing than your words. When you preach, what you do with your body and the expression on your face is often going to speak more loudly than your words. Whatever your situation when you come to preach, be it one of gravity or levity, your sadness or joy is going to be communicated much more by your comportment than by what you are saying. We must take care how we appear to others. How often has someone said to you in passing 'Cheer up, it's not that bad' and you've been surprised because you felt quite good that day. I suppose I speak from personal experience here because although quite often I am feeling fine inside it seems that my face doesn't always betray that feeling to others. I don't think it is because I have a sad face so much as the fact that I am often preoccupied and my mind is concentrating on other matters at the time.

I had the experience once of a hilarious, while at the same time rather sad, example of this. I had occasion to attend the funeral of a close relative near my paternal home in Scotland. It is a custom in those parts when somebody is being buried, for senior members of the family in decreasing order of seniority to be responsible for holding a cord to let the coffin down into the grave. On this occasion the person in charge had decided to break with tradition and get the young grandsons to do it. Unfortunately the situation got the better of them. It may have been embarrassment at being asked to do such an important job or they may have found it funny in a grotesque sort of way, whatever the reason they all stood there with silly grins on their faces as they lowered the coffin into the grave. This was a very serious moment and of course their reaction made everyone else feel extremely put out. Afterwards they said they had not been laughing, which was probably true, but their faces had seemed to tell a different story. How often does that sort of thing happen in other contexts? I have heard ministers standing in the pulpit talking about the joy of the resurrection of Jesus, but speaking about it in such a monotonous and dried up way that you would never think it was the most explosive thing that has ever happened on the face of the earth.

Examples of Non-Verbal Communication

(a) *Eye contact*

Eye contact is essential for effective communication. I studied under a particular professor who was a great writer and an amazing scholar, but his lectures bored me, and everyone else around me, to death. He lectured looking out of the window, reading from notes that he'd prepared twenty years before, while drumming his fingers on the desk. We could just as well have sat and read what he'd written, rather than have to suffer this awful non-communication. It's vital to get over the embarrassment of looking people in the eye. This is especially true when we're dealing with a particular personal revelation. God may bring a word that is not only a general word of preaching, but has particular relevance to one person. It may not be apparent at the time, but perhaps years later it will become evident that the person you made eye contact with at that moment was the very person to whom God wanted to speak in that moment in a very direct way. If, however, you never look at anyone but only at some anonymous space in the distance then the directness of the word will be lost.

(b) Diction

Here we are concerned not so much with the words that are used but whether they are enunciated clearly or not. As a Scotsman this is of especial interest to me. Many years ago I was sent to elocution lessons. Some who know me personally will no doubt be surprised at this fact. They may be even more surprised to learn that after only two lessons or so my tutor told me not to bother to come any more. He said that I could not, nor should I try to, get rid of my Scots accent, and that I was already doing the things that were necessary to good communication. I pronounced my 'd's and 't's, had good diction, got the points of emphasis and the correct reading and I did not mumble. There was a time when all over the world people thought it was necessary to speak BBC English to communicate properly, but these days we recognise much more the importance of keeping the colour and the interest that comes with having an accent from a particular region or country. W.E. Sangster, one of the greatest British preachers, was an up-graded Cockney. He didn't get rid of his accent. He refined it so that what people wouldn't understand was taken away. The rest he played upon and used the peculiarities of it to great effect.

(c) Tone

A voice is like an instrument. Depending on how we alter the tone, the emphasis – hard, soft, fast, slow – alters the way in which the words are communicated. There are so many different ways in which even a simple word can be used. Take the word 'yes', for example. The way someone says 'yes' tells you a whole lot about how they really feel. Ask a question and get a firm 'yes' in reply, and it communicates trust or confidence. Ask the same question to someone else and if they respond with a drawn-out, hesitant 'y...e...s', that seems to have spaces between the letters, the impression is transmitted immediately that although they are using the affirmative there is probably an unspoken 'but' in their reply.

(d) Gestures

It has been said of many of the best communicators that if their hands were cut off they couldn't speak. Of course, there is a danger of overplaying gestures. True communication does, however, involve the whole body as we've seen. Personal and physical involvement is often what gives life and dynamism to the message of the preacher and teacher. The dynamic reality of the truth of God's word has to be true in our lives first before we can communicate it to others, and if it's true to us then we're going to display it. Paul said that he was compelled to preach God's word. I find it hard to imagine someone feeling like that inside and, at the same time, standing outwardly rigid like a plank of wood before his audience. This is not something that can be worked up in an artificial way. Some people are more flamboyant in their gestures than others, because that reflects their personality, but for effective personal communication people must see the signs of life in us when we speak to them.

A Voice From the Past

The orators of Ancient Rome practised and perfected the art of communication in a way that has much to teach us. When they delivered public orations they followed a number of formal styles which reflected the intention of their speech. These styles are reflected in the three Latin words used to describe them:

(1) *'placere'* – in English this is akin to the word 'placate', which means to please to the point of removing any displeasure. This is not exactly how it was applied in oratory. The Roman orator didn't set out to gain favour with his audience in that way, but to please them by 'gripping' them with his words. David Watson always taught the people who were with him on mission to 'pray for grip.' There has got to be 'grip'. You can see that *'placere'* then becomes a very active word. We have to be active – as preachers and teachers we are responsible for the grip or lack of it.

(2) *'docere'* – this means to teach or bring enlightenment. As we've said before, there's no point in standing up to speak if we have no content to what we're saying. Otherwise we'll be like disused windmills on a windy day – thrashing the air with lots of action and noise, but no meaning.

(3) *'movere'* – to move, or motivate. The Romans spoke of 'moving the heart.' What we have to say has to pass through all other points of intellect and taste until it reaches **the** point, so that people will be moved. We must always ask ourselves what we intend to achieve through this particular communication in the minds and hearts of our listeners. And is it achieving that? Sangster tells us somewhere of a preacher who was well renowned for the fact that he 'aimed at nothing and hit it.' We need to know the aim of our communication.

Firstly then, the communicator needs to grip the attention of the audience; then bring enlightenment to them through the content of the message; then through the power of words that reach the heart and life move them onwards. It seems a straightforward process when set out like this. Why, therefore, do we fail so often? The truth is if we applied these simple and direct principles to our communication they would make a radical difference to its effect.

Chapter 6

Personal Questions

In this chapter I want to look at two subjects which are of vital importance to good communication. The first I have called **personal factors** which is about the areas of our personal life and habitat which affect for good or ill the way other people receive what we have to say. The second is the question of **presentation**, because a good subject badly shared can come across much worse than a poor subject well shared. Often we live and act quite oblivious to the impressions we leave with other people. With regard to communication this is very important because sometimes the credibility of the message can be quite blighted by the failure of the one communicating it to take certain very basic essentials into consideration. If it is true that as Christian communicators we are handling the greatest themes in the world, then surely they deserve the best attention we can give them in every area.

1. Personal Factors

I accept, of course, that questions of taste and culture affect to a large degree our appreciation of what is appropriate in any given situation. It would also be true to say that expectations have changed drastically over the past few years within Christian circles. Not too long ago it would have been out of the question to go to any meeting in casual clothes and certainly the speaker would have been expected to dress rather more formally for the occasion. Nowadays almost anything goes. Some might think the pendulum has swung too much in the opposite direction.

(a) Appearance

As we have just noted the question of dress is a tricky one in today's context. There seem to be no set rules today and there are so many different styles around. Whether we like it or not, people judge us by our appearance, so we do need to have a set of standards.

Of course, the context within which one is speaking will determine the style and level of dress to a large extent. As a person who is involved in a great deal of travelling ministry I find myself in many different contexts from one meeting to the next. For example, I was taken aback the first time I went to minister in Africa. The temperature was over 100 degrees and I had taken cool, short sleeved, open-necked shirts and lightweight trousers. To my horror I discovered that they expected me to preach in a formal suit, dress shirt and tie. I was melted before I'd even started! After many more visits they have come to know me and we have reached a happy compromise. The important point to note is the fact that had I insisted on what I thought was right on that first occasion, I may not have been asked back, however powerful the word I preached.

Some, of course, may recoil from such considerations on the protest that where the Spirit of the Lord is there is liberty, which means we can do what we like. Well, I agree that there are times when tradition needs to be challenged. After all, if the question of dress has become an idol or a dead religious tradition then part of our prophetic task may be to address such issues. That is not the point I am trying to make. The point is this. We are meant to be handling the greatest message the world has ever heard. Can we afford to do this in such a manner that may in fact prevent other people from hearing and receiving the word of God through the channel of our person?

I must say on a wider spectrum that I do get upset when I see how people attend the word of God. We have travelled so far away from the old traditions of dress and respect that we are in danger of our personal appearance being so casual on a Sunday morning that we give the impression of not really caring too much about attendance to God's things anyway. This was brought home to me on one occasion when I was invited as guest of honour at an anniversary celebration in a 'new' church. On the Saturday night the fellowship met together for a dinner in a local hall. The setting was fantastic, the food excellent and everybody was dressed to kill. The ladies with their best evening dress and the men with suits and ties. The next morning the same people met to worship and as I stood up to speak to them I had to look twice to check they were the same group of people. Many of them looked as though they had just fallen out of bed and grabbed the first item of casual clothing to wear to church. It caused me to think.

When I preach I try to judge what will be comfortable and appropriate. For example, speaking under a lot of lights can become very uncomfortable if you are wearing clothes which are too heavy. Some may think this a trivial subject, but there is a fine line between the physical and spiritual and in an area like this it is surprising how one can affect the other quite radically. The medium may not be the message, but the medium certainly affects the message to a great degree.

(b) Personal hygiene

This is another most important area. Ministry often involves encounters of the close kind! Bad breath, tooth decay, body odour, smelly clothes, greasy hair, dirty collars, unkempt or dirty finger nails, can all prove a great stumbling-block to the person being ministered to. Church buildings have changed greatly in style today and communication does not take place so much with the speaker raised up on a podium speaking from or across such a distance. A great deal of modern communication takes place at or near the same level as the audience. Also, it is quite common for the speaker to be in close proximity to people before or after a meeting. In Corinthians Paul describes us *'the fragrance of Christ'*; it might surprise us what sort of fragrance other people get when we are close to them! With apologies to Paul it can have a very strong and sometimes adverse affect on how they receive the message.

The gospel should have an effect on the body as well as on the brain and spirit. There's no virtue in smelling bad! When we communicate our hands tend to be very visible. There is really no excuse for dirty or unkempt finger nails. My father was a coal-miner who had to face the challenge of ingrained coal dust; yet when he preached in church on a Sunday you would have thought he worked in the local bank, so clean were his hands.

Clean clothes, clean hands, sweet-smelling bodies – we should not have to mention these things yet there can be a sort of twisted psyche in some Christians that says: 'I'm too busy with the important things of God to be concerned with things like this' ... Get concerned! These are things that affect our communication of God's word. Of course we must also be careful not to go too much in the other direction. We have to maintain a happy balance. On the one hand there must not be the offence of the unclean, on the other, the sort of show of fashion and style which detracts from the gospel. Above all, be comfortable. Be at ease with your dress and feel good in yourself, because if you are comfortable and feel good then others will feel good and comfortable with you.

No smoking

This is another important matter. If you smoke, quite bluntly, you shouldn't.

Paul put his finger on it when he said to the Corinthians:

> *'Do you not know that your body is a temple of the Holy Spirit, who is in you, whom you have received from God?'*
> (1 Corinthians 6:19)

I have heard the objection that famous preachers like Charles Haddon Spurgeon, the great Baptist preacher of last century smoked a pipe. Usually such objections are raised by people who, in other areas of their lives, couldn't hold a candle to men like Spurgeon as far as passion for the gospel and holiness of life are concerned. My father used to put it in his own pithy way when he reminded such objectors that 'Many smake like Spurgeon but few spake like him.'

In any case, we have discovered so many negative things since Spurgeon's day about tobacco. We know it has a disastrously detrimental effect on the human body. It's a degenerate thing. The fug that it leaves around, and on the person, is a total repellent in ministry. We do need smoke, but of the kind with which God filled the temple, not that which comes from stale cigarettes. Of course, others go on to object vociferously about their personal liberty. This is the cry of the age. I am afraid the words which close the text we referred to from 1 Corinthians 6:19 would not be voted flavour of the month amongst some Christians today. Paul goes on to remind us so simply and clearly:

'You are not your own; you were bought at a price.'

(c) Personality traits

Have you ever wondered how you really do appear in the eyes of other people? Anyone who takes on the role of communicating in public, must be willing to subject themselves to some personal scrutiny as far as their audience is concerned. Personal mannerisms can easily become an ingrained part of how we speak and act. If it is any consolation let me say that we all have them – these quirks in our personality and presentation! However, when someone else sees and hears us for the first time those quirks and mannerisms may be the very things that get in the way of our communicating with them. So it is important to recognize these things.

This does not mean however, we should always get rid of

all the unique little mannerisms or ways of speaking we have. There are times when these things can be used to great effect and can become a strength rather than a hindrance in our communication. The question is whether it is a nuisance or an unnecessary quirk, because it can then be the source of a great distraction to our audience. Take, for example, the habit of quite a few preachers who spend quite a part of their time hitching up their trousers. If they saw themselves they would be surprised at the frequency of the habit. It may be a sign of an inner lack of confidence. Whatever the cause I cannot imagine that it adds anything useful to the subject in hand. It is better to overcome the habit and find something more useful to do with our hands.

(d) Habitat

So often a person's true nature is reflected in where and how they live. On the surface they may look neat and tidy in their dress but if the habitat in which they live is one of disorder and uncleanliness, sooner or later this will reflect at some point in their public ministry. It may be covered up with smart clothes, but eventually something from the untidiness of the normal habitat will betray itself, maybe through untidiness of mind, language, manner or spirit, but somehow or other it will show itself in how we speak and share.

Ministry calls for discipline and personal training. These things usually start, not in public, but in the private and deeply personal areas of our lives. We must not become stumbling blocks to other people being able to receive the word of God through us. What Paul says is so important, *'We do not preach ourselves, but Jesus Christ as Lord'* (2 Corinthians 4:5). Just think of the stumbling blocks Paul had to get over at a personal level. It seems from how he speaks to the Galatians that he had bad eyesight; according to other traditions he was either bald, hunch-backed or bow-legged! According to Paul himself he had a *'thorn in the flesh'* and his appearance was not the best in his own opinion. Yet more power came through Paul in the gospel than any man has exercised on the face of the earth. He knew how to let himself diminish and let the power of God come through.

These are only a few issues we need to face at a personal level but if we do then, with God's help, we will become more effective and acceptable to others as we share with them the word of Life.

2. Presentation

The second major area which calls for discipline on the part of all of us who aspire to preach the gospel or teach the people of God concerns the question of how we present what we have to say. It never ceases to amaze me that Christians are so sloppy in this regard. In the world of business and the professions this is one area which is regarded with a sense of its importance. There is no getting away from the fact that how the message is communicated greatly affects how it is received or perhaps whether it is received at all. In this age of charismatic enthusiasm it has become accepted in some circles that no preparation of subject or mind is really necessary. Some vague allusion is made to the fact that Jesus told us not to worry about what we should say because in that day it would be given to us. A fairly cursory reading of the text in question will lead us to the conclusion that what Jesus was talking about was something entirely different from the call and demand to teach and preach the gospel in the way of which we are speaking in this book. The result of this is, of course, patently clear to see. In many parts of the Body of Christ there is an alarming and increasing ignorance of the revelation of God, and an inability on the part of many to give a reason for the hope that is in them. Such a move in the end leads to the saddest of all states amongst the people of God, namely, a total lack of discernment in relation to truth and a growing gullibility which accepts anything which sounds spiritual and promises great blessing and power.

Let's consider a few areas in relation to the presentation of our material which are important.

(a) Grasp of the subject

Before I entered full-time ministry I worked for a large pharmaceutical house. Part of my job was to present new preparations to medical staff in general practice and in hospital. I can recall those moments quite clearly when I felt really good about the job and about my presentations. Those were the times when I had taken the trouble to get a good grasp of my subject. I had read up on the research, I was very familiar with the characteristics of the preparation in question and was well prepared for any questions that might be thrown at me about its use and application. Equally well I remember times when this was not the case. At those times one went into interviews with a sense of caution and uncertainty, and there was not the same feeling of confidence about the situation.

The same is true in any communicative context and particularly so in the realm of Christian communication. Spiritual confidence is engendered by an inward assurance about the subject. Embarrassment, lack of conviction, a feeling of failure and many other emotions can result from the failure of preparation of mind and spirit. I am not suggesting that every talk we give needs to be based on academic study, or that we all need to be theologically equipped at a profound level. There are, however, at least two things we should always do. The first is to make sure that we have reflected enough on what we want to say so that we are clear of the content, shape and purpose of it. The second needs only a little research or study to ensure that we are not about to make a terrible gaffe and produce some heresy without us knowing it. We need not imagine that this does not happen. Far better known preachers than we might ever be, have fallen into these traps only to suffer unnecessary embarrassment themselves and to cause needless confusion amongst the listeners.

This is a challenge, I believe, to evangelists in particular. Some people imagine that evangelism is the easy option of Christian communication. How wrong they are! I find evangelistic preaching the most challenging of all. It demands that every time a statement is made about the gospel it has to be backed up with other reserves of knowledge and spiritual understanding. There's no such thing as 'simple evangelism'. The best evangelists can make it sound simple, but they are usually those with the most profound grasp of the subject. The more a person knows his subject the clearer is his communication of it. To make a gospel statement simple, you need to have a wider grasp of the subject from a personal, biblical and theological point of view than might be revealed by the words which are used at the time. Unfortunately, evangelism which grows out of deep experience and profound understanding is largely lost today. It has been replaced with superficiality.

Simplicity versus superficiality

There's all the difference in the world between simplicity and superficiality. The gift of simplicity comes from two sources for the Christian speaker. First, of course, we would identify the anointing of God; there is a given-ness about the ability to communicate something that is hard to grasp and make it simple to the hearer. The gospel is not easy to understand at a natural level. It's about deep things. The second source of simplicity is understanding. The preacher who knows what he believes, who has taken time to reflect and apply himself to the essence of his message and is anointed in the power of the Holy Spirit, is able to make these deep things reachable by other men and women who listen. Knowing something through and through requires time and commitment. Some speakers sound as though they know a great deal, but something that is superficial has no reservoir of understanding behind it.

Every time we open our mouths and make any statement with regard to Christian belief and life, we are immediately involving ourselves with the whole gospel.

Firstly, therefore, we need to know something of the context out of which our current statements extend. Secondly, we also have to be able to make some value judgements about the veracity of our claims. Unless we operate with some wider understanding of the gospel, we might find our-selves speaking rubbish without recognizing the fact.

Anyone with the ambition to be an effective spiritual com-municator faces these sorts of challenges:
– The challenge of developing our understanding of the subject we handle which is the glorious gospel of Christ.
– The challenge of getting to grips with our theme every time we speak, so that we can utter it with confidence and clarity.
– The challenge of being able to handle themes which are hidden to the natural mind and opening them out in such a way that the simplest amongst our hearers, receives something of the bread of life on which to feed.
This, in fact, is the true authority of the preacher.

Another lesson we need to learn is not to be fooled by people who appear to speak 'off the cuff'. Seeming spon-taneity usually rises from two sources; one is a lifetime of experience and preparation after which the word is burned in the mind and heart and it takes no great effort to call it to mind. The other is the depth of a profound experience of God in which the testimony of what God has done is so real that it takes very little effort to bring it to mind. In both cases the word can flow with ease, one born out of applica-tion, the other out of the white heat of real experience. All of us have either experienced this or seen it in action. It is dangerous, however, to try and copy either without the ful-filment of the necessary qualifications and neither of these comes cheaply. I am not saying that the Holy Spirit cannot or will not ever inspire an immediate word through someone who is unprepared. That is patently not the case. However, no one can sustain a meaningful ministry of the Word on that principle for very long.

(b) Personal effects

The second area to consider in relation to our presentation is what I have called personal effects. By this I mean the impressions we give by our physical presence in the event.

Let me pick out just a few points of interest:

– stance and posture

We say a lot by how we stand. How many times have you seen a preacher, hunched over a lectern and muttering into the wood? Those who are communicating spiritual truths should stand tall in the gospel! Lift your head and look at people. Demonstrate by your stance that this is a gospel worth speaking about. And you can stand tall whatever your height. Charles Simeon was a great preacher of the past. He was so short-sighted that he had to stand with a candle in one hand and read from a manuscript. Charles Simeon was spiritually tall, however, and in the anointing of God overcame his disabilities and inhibitions and became one of the most powerful preachers of his day.

– speech

Language, like dress is far from uniform and an accent can add a great deal to a person's speech. However, we must remember that the object of our ministry is to communicate the word of God in a clear way. There is no virtue in using accent for its own sake, but neither is there any virtue in suppressing it and sounding forced and artificial.

– reading

Any effective spiritual communicator needs to learn how to read the Bible with effect so its depth of meaning and power is released to the listener. Proper reading of the Scriptures aloud is something that seems to have gone by the board these days. I had the privilege of being brought up with the public reading of the Scriptures. At Sunday school we had competitions to see who could learn a piece and speak it out to the best effect. I understand that this will seem quaint and perhaps old-fashioned to many but it was the foundation of my desire and ability to speak in public. Often when I listen to Scripture being read today I feel that the art of reading in public has been lost. Yet Paul said to Timothy,

> *'Devote yourself to the public reading of the scripture, to preaching and to teaching.'* (1 Timothy 4:13)

There's all the difference in the world between a Bible reading and the Bible being read properly. What I am advocating is that the Bible be read as part of the whole process of communication. When the Scriptures are read in this way their real meaning and power stands out for all to see. Often what is said afterwards is little more than an underscoring of what has already been made plain in the reading of the text. I am not arguing for a stiff liturgical rendering in which artificial tones are used but for a spiritual release of the word of God in Scripture. This can have an amazing effect on an audience who perhaps have never read the text in this way for themselves. It does help if we first practise reading a passage out loud. Take note of the sentences and how they are constructed. Look at the passages around the particular text you want to emphasize or perhaps preach from; see how it fits into its context. This will greatly enhance your own understanding and appreciation of the text and may throw even greater light on it as you pay attention to these things. English verse numbers and chapter divisions don't always tell the whole truth about a passage. Get the beat of the Scripture and read it to its beat. Then people will understand what they're listening to and enter into it far more readily.

For myself I love the public reading of Scripture. There are spiritual skills which badly need to be recovered today so that people may receive and understand the Word of God in a fresh and dynamic way. The Word of God needs to become a living reality in the minds and then in the hearts and lives of people. If that doesn't happen then we have failed to totally communicate the gospel of life.

(c) Places and people

Preaching takes place in a context. That context is of the people listening and the place in which they are listening. To communicate effectively, we need to handle the context both in people terms and place terms. Sometimes the people or the place or both can overpower the preacher. There's a saying among actors that it's dangerous to do a film with children or animals because they always steal the show. It can be the same with preaching! At one meeting some time ago I had to compete with a hand-held computer game. Every time I made a point, it made a point. Although the subject in hand was not spiritual warfare it might have been more appropriate if it had been since we had all the sound effects right there. Children no doubt are a great blessing from the Lord, but there are times when they can be a real distraction. In the old days children were seen and not heard in church meetings to such a degree that many of those same children grew up in rebellion against every memory of the faith of their parents. Nevertheless there are times when steps need to be taken positively to improve the situation. In this particular case I had to suggest to the mother that the child be taken out with the toy for its benefit and ours. Quite a radical step in our *avant garde* times but the ensuing silence was a great blessing to everyone. The lesson – be in control of the situation.

– the audience

I like to get a look at the audience before I have to start speaking to them. This helps me to assess them. The Holy Spirit is able to help see into our audience and perceive the state of their hearts and minds long before we say a word to them. It is useful to be able to put a spiritual finger on the hot spots, the cold spots, the bored spots, the troubled spots. I like to have some sort of spiritual summary in my own spirit of this body of people I have been asked to address because this will undoubtedly affect the way I approach them. I like to meet them in spirit before I address them in words. It is even possible to achieve a good level of insight with a very sizeable crowd. This unspoken communication is, I believe, of great significance in the practise of effective communication.

– distractions

There are three main ways to handle distractions. The first is wherever possible to make light of them and the second is to put people at their ease. For example, take the common situation of someone who starts coughing. We all know from bitter experience that a simple cough can turn very quickly into an apoplectic fit if it's suppressed. The answer is not always in the laying on of hands for spiritual healing but more often in friendly reassurance and the offer of a glass of water. This leads on to the third principle – deal with the situation in a straightforward manner. Exercise control and a firm hand where necessary. In all things we must remember that we are there to minister the Word of God. Whatever we do with distractions, we have to display a servant attitude; even though our actions may need to be strong and clear at times.

Better take the risk of one offended than a thousand misled.

– flexibility

Imagine a situation where you arrive to speak at a meeting only to discover that the mood and context is totally different from what you had expected. What do you do? Some preachers would carry on regardless on the premise that the Lord had given them the word and that He must know best. I would argue that this is a situation in which we quickly need to learn the lesson of flexibility. I remember one occasion when I had agreed to give a Saturday evening talk. It was to be at the end of a regional 'fun day' for a particular denomination. When the time came to speak it was very clear that the fun day had been so successful that the last thing the people wanted was the 'great word from the Lord' that I had come prepared to give.

God gives words for the moment but He is also far more flexible than we tend to be and He can easily lead us to another far more appropriate word for an occasion such as this. In the event this is exactly what happened. Because of a willingness to flex with the situation, God was able to speak in such a way that connected with the mood of the people and left them with a word which really spoke into the situation in a way that my previously prepared talk never would have done. Now I realise that such flexibility grows with practice. It is, however, something that is worth the practice because it means that we can, in Pauline terms, become all things to all men that by some means we might win some.

A measure of wisdom is needed in all these things. The presentation of our message is important, after all we are carrying a message from the King of kings! This does not, however, mean that we have licence to behave like a prima donna. It simply means that we must ensure that to the best of our ability we will make the conditions as good as possible for the word to go out. Sometimes, however, it does prove impossible to change the externals. Then there is only one alternative – we must change. It comes down to a question of flexibility again. If, for example, the stage lighting is so strong that it cuts out any possibility of seeing the audience from the stage or platform then don't worry about it too much. Take comfort in the thought that although you cannot connect directly with them the very same lighting means that the audience can connect with you very powerfully.

Some communicators get so bound by external difficulties that they become very restricted in their effectiveness. We need to pray that God will help us to overcome the elements which threaten to hinder us at the physical, personal and practical levels. Then we can be free and more effective in our communication of this tremendous, dynamic, living gospel that we've been given to share in the name of Jesus.

Chapter 7

Workmen Approved

'Do your best to present yourself to God as one approved; a workman who does not need to be ashamed and who correctly handles the word of truth.'

(2 Timothy 2:15)

Those words first addressed to Timothy are fundamental to the success of any spiritual communication. One reason for this is the fact that some people never attempt to share their faith to any degree because they fear they have nothing worthwhile to say or because they feel totally ill-equipped through lack of formal training or theological education. It is no doubt true that, in general, we have witnessed a radical decline in biblical awareness and ability and that many of the foundations which could be taken for granted years ago because of parental influence or Sunday School training have vanished in the main. On the other hand the past few decades have seen the growing phenomenon of thousands upon thousands of new believers who, while not enjoying the benefits of a deep Christian heritage, nevertheless, do show a new level of keenness to learn and be open to the things of God for themselves. This is one of the strong grounds for hope in the present generation. If the many new Christian believers can be encouraged, excited and equipped in the things of God there is a good potential for growth and development in these areas.

So let's not be too discouraged at the seeming lack of technical expertise. After all it is not quite clear how much of it the early disciples had and they became known as 'those who turned the world upside down'! Rather, let's take a look at what we have got and more than that what we might have with just a little application. Because that is what the Scriptures enjoin us to do. They challenge us to do our best and to apply ourselves with the help of the Spirit of God so that we might grow, not only in grace, but in our ability to share the good things of God with those around us.

Just as in any other area of enterprise, we need to consider carefully the resources which are available to us. What can we draw on? The answer is, on the one hand much more straightforward that we might imagine, and on the other much more profound than we might imagine. I want to look at **five important areas** which provide us with resources with which to fulfil the task.

1. Our Experience of God

In his Epistle John highlights the significance of this fact. He tells his readers:

> *'That which was from the beginning, which we have heard, which we have seen with our eyes, which we have looked at and our hands have touched – this we proclaim concerning the Word of life.'* (1 John 1:1)

Now, no doubt John had a very special experience of the personal glory of Jesus. He had the privilege of being on the mountain top and seeing something tremendous of the revelation of the glory of God through Him. Nevertheless the principle holds good for us in our own measure. The revelation of God is communicated through human experience and the further we move historically away from the early beginnings of Christian testimony the more this needs to be the case.

Of course, we don't necessarily always preach about

experience but we need to speak from experience. Our experience of God is a very important source as far as our ability to communicate is concerned. Some of us no doubt need to learn to understand our own experience more deeply. Usually our experience of God is far deeper and broader than we would imagine. This is an area that we need to let the Holy Spirit exercise our minds about. We need to understand our experiences; to understand the central issues of spirituality in them. This is one area which I have found to be of utmost significance in my own ministry. I have discovered that implanted within some of my experiences of God have been principles of life which have stood out and which the Spirit of God has enabled me to gather together to explain to other people. In this sense our personal experience of God is a gold-mine of revelation for the benefit of others and a profitable resource for our ministry. In fact, I would go further. It seems to me that God, by His working in our lives, implants in our experience many of the principles that will become the governing principles of our ministry.

Experience does count for something! Don't make the mistake of discounting your experience and thinking that someone else's must be more valuable. God has given each one of us a very real and personal experience through our encounters with Him. We need to reflect more on these experiences, not just have them and let them slip away. We need to learn to meditate on our experiences and to align them with Scripture, so that we can begin to see the divine principles in them. For example, I've usually found that people who are evangelists will find that in the background of their encounter with God there are experiences that uniquely point forwards to their becoming evangelists. Having experience is a tremendous reservoir of resource for our preaching or teaching.

2. Our Acquaintance with Life

If we were to take a poll of all the people who read this book we would discover a vast and multi-varied experience of life.

Each of us knows, in our own measure, what life is about. Of course there are some people who never quite seem to grasp that or learn its lessons. In the main, however, we do get to know people and how they tick; we become acquainted with life and its circumstances. We live life, and we meet lots of people who don't know the saving power of Jesus. In short, life is a great reservoir of resource for our preaching and teaching. This is particularly the case when it comes to the question of illustrating the truth. Illustration needs to be a living thing, so the first thing it needs to be is personal; not just borrowed from somebody else. How many times does the same illustration seem to be used by different speakers to the point that, not only is the audience bored, but the story has completely lost its point and power. There has to be a livingness about what we say and that comes from our acquaintance with life.

At theological college we were taught to cull our illustrations from everything we ever read; books, magazines, quotations; all were stored away in our card-index system with studious care to be brought out at the appropriate moment to illustrate some theological point in the latest sermon. Now I am not at all decrying order and purpose in our reading. However, I will take the risk of saying that history has demonstrated how dull and unrelated to real life such an exercise can become. If we use a literary quotation, which I often do, it must be used with life. Reference to it must come in some personal way which carries interest within it. It must not be a quote just dug out to suit the moment.

The point I am making is simple. Every one of our lives is a walking encyclopedia of God's grace and goodness and a living illustration of His dealings with us and our response to Him. There can be no more living illustration of the truth than this.

3. Our Knowledge of People

Human life is not lived in isolation, at least it's not meant to be. Every one of us have friends, relatives, people we work with and so on. This means that intuitively we build up our own understanding of all sorts of different people. We learn how they act and react, what makes them tick. We recognise the ones we get along with more easily and those who present us with personal challenges. Our communicating the gospel is relative to all of this. It is for people!

It is our knowledge of people and their needs that contextualizes our preaching and makes it relevant to those who hear. It is our personal insight into people and their needs which provides an effective forum for our preaching. Any living, relevant word which we speak operates between two poles; on the one hand, the revelation of the Spirit of God, on the other the lives of those to whom we bring the word. The spark of life bridges the gap and brings power and vitality through the word into the hearts and lives of our hearers.

4. Our Fellowship with Other Minds

The first three areas of resource we have looked at arise from the daily practice of our lives because we are involved with them naturally day by day. This sadly is not the case with this fourth example. This is the resource which is open to us all in our interaction with the thoughts and experience of other servants of God through the medium of print, tape and video. Sadly, many miss the opportunity through lack of application and the development of basic skills of reading and listening in a fruitful way. Over the years I have tried to practise reading the lives and testimonies of other men and women of God as well as reading the sort of books which develop my mind and imagination and provide insight on many spiritual issues. Over the years I have found great value in living within the written word of testimony brought by other men and women of God. To understand how they saw things, what they said, what they felt. We live in an age of instant communication and, although I make teaching videos myself, I feel that one major down side of video and telecommunication is that it cuts people off from the slower and more personally-involved arena of entering into the thoughts and lives of other people that comes through their written word. I can testify that what has helped me most in communicating to others has been this fellowship with other minds greater than my own. In fact, we ourselves may not be great people according to the world's view of greatness, but what a privilege we have to be able to walk with some of the spiritual giants through their writings and speaking! It is likely that we never knew them or met them in the flesh. If they were alive today we might never be in a position to meet them personally. Through their writings, however, as God's Spirit illuminates the meaning of what they say, we can have fellowship with their minds and spirits.

5. Our Understanding of the Scriptures

It would seem obvious that if we have a desire to share the word of God then we need to develop a deep, personal acquaintance with the Scriptures. Paul reminds us in Scriptures like Romans 15:4 how much benefit there is to be gained from our acquaintance with the Scriptures.

> *'Everything that was written in the past was written to teach us so that through endurance and the encouragement of the Scriptures we might have hope.'*

This does not seem as clear to other people as it does to the present writer. Many pay lip service to the Bible but in practice all they do is use it as a sort of divine promise box. No doubt the Scriptures contain many thousands of promises but anyone with the ambition to speak God's word for today will need to operate with a much deeper understanding of the Scriptures than this.

Of course, some seem to have become bored with the Bible. Perhaps the fault here lies at the hands of preachers they have heard who have failed to transmit the life and power which the Scriptures contain. There's no need to be bored with the Bible! I confess to being bored sometimes with traditional approaches to Bible reading and study but over the years I have developed an increasing awareness of the sheer variety within the Scriptures. The Scriptures operate at so many different levels of interest. I have found the Bible to be a source of amazing interest and variety, from profound spiritual insight to intriguing literary twist. God has provided His revelation in such a marvellous interweave of the hidden and the obvious, the divine and the human, the time-conditioned and the eternal.

We need to get rid of our boredom about the Bible and begin to be excited about the Scriptures. When we come to them we are like gold miners digging for tremendous resources: a personal release of the word of God into our hearts and from there into the lives of other men and women. They don't want dead beat stuff. They don't want vain repetition. They don't even want just a repetition of the words of the Bible! What they want is a revelation of the word of God. A tremendous interaction takes place between the word of God through Scripture and the witness of the Holy Spirit in the heart of the believer as he or she waits before God for the living word. Of all the resources that are available to anyone who wants to share God's word today the chief source must be the Scriptures inspired and released into our minds and hearts through the influence of the Holy Spirit.

If we are to appreciate the proper place of the Scriptures in our communication of the faith there are a number of basic, but important, factors we should consider. Among these will be:

(a) The question of our familiarity with the Word

The simple fact is that we are never going to get the word out of Scripture, unless we have a daily openness to and familiarity with the Scriptures. By this I don't just mean reading a verse here and there to get a blessing. Some people use the Bible the way other people use those little Christian promise boxes – they open it up looking for a 'word' for the moment and if they don't like the first choice they pass quickly on to another. There is an awful and, I am sure, apocryphal story about one man who did just that and turned up the phrase, 'Judas went out and hanged himself.' He didn't think much of that as a blessing so turned the page and the word leapt out at him, 'Go and do thou likewise.'

It is at moments like this that I thank God for my own spiritual upbringing. As a young teenager I had to learn to name the books of the Bible straight off. Learning things 'parrot fashion' may not be in line with modern teaching philosophy, but the fact is that much later when I came to study theology I didn't have to think twice about where the Bible was in relation to itself. When I learned biblical history I learned, for example, that the book of Chronicles was not written at the same time as the book of Kings, but comes from the period of the return from exile for the Jews. Although it repeats the same body of material historically, it's written from a different perspective to revitalise the hopes of the exiled people coming back into the land. When I learnt that it did two things for me. One, it answered the question I'd had when young as to why Chronicles was slightly different from Kings. Two, because I knew how both books ran in the text, I had no problem attaching a date to it. Then one became a sort of memory aid for the other.

Ignorance of the fundamental structures and emphases of the Scriptures hinders, I believe, the capacity of many Christians to receive and retain the wonders of biblical revelation and even to tackle some of the apparent difficulties we come across in our study of the Bible.

Today we are in danger of unfettered subjectivism where every idea and notion is labelled God's word without the benefit of the sort of discernment and control that comes with a deeper knowledge and understanding of the Scriptures.

(b) The question of our study of the Word

The second thing we need to develop is some sort of systematic approach to our reading and study of the Scriptures. This, above all, will save us from the rather haphazard approach we may have indulged in until now.

Firstly, different versions of the Bible

Some people find the vast range of new translations more of a hindrance than a help. However, for someone who wants to study the Scriptures in a helpful and positive way this cannot be the case. I know there are some who believe that the Authorised Version carries an authenticity of translation that others don't. A brief examination of the history of translation and an experiment in the comparison of terminology will show this not to be the case. Of course, every version has a bias but if we see this and take it into account we will find that a study which encompasses more than one translation will prove more beneficial than one which sticks only to a well loved version.

When I go to the Scriptures to prepare something or even to read casually, I never use just one version. There are many different versions these days and much argument concerning them. In the main though, the NIV (New International Version) is a trustworthy and reliable version. You may like to use the New King James. Of course, the older King James reflects the tremendous glory of classical English, but its terminology and expression are really too far removed from the modern mind and understanding to be helpful. We have to remember that as Christians we may be familiar with things that other people are lost with. To be effective a communicator does not just stand on his own ground, he has to stand on other people's ground as well. Let me recommend to you the J.B. Phillips version of the New Testament. In the 1950s and 60s J.B. Phillips, an Anglican vicar, translated the New Testament. It is more a paraphrase than a strict translation, but what a paraphrase! It lives and breathes with dynamic vitality. The light that comes from reading a version like this alongside your normal translation is tremendous.

Secondly, Bible helps

Chief amongst these must be a good concordance. A concordance lists in order the main Bible words with their meanings and occurrences and cross references. Modern concordances tend to be generated by computer but person-ally I still like to use my old Young's concordance. I find that this old fashioned concordance seems to have a much greater depth than some of the newer offerings. Perhaps it has something to do with the fact that it is the product of a whole lifetime of personal study and hard work. The draw-back with something like Young's is that it calls for some familiarity with the Authorised Version, but if you use that or the NKJ alongside your NIV you can recapture the words quite easily.

A concordance can also be very useful in giving some idea of the original Hebrew and Greek words which lie behind the English text. This does not require the user to be fluent in the ancient languages, but it can often lead to a clearer or greater understanding of the meaning of the words which the Scriptures use. Surely this must be of tremendous benefit to our communication. Sometimes, for example, a concordance can help us to see that one word in English may actually reflect four or more different words in the original lan-guages. An outstanding example is the word 'sin'. Research in a concordance will demonstrate the real breadth and depth of the subject from a biblical point of view and, instead of being left with some dead, moralistic idea of the subject, it will show the sheer mobility and dynamic rele-vance of biblical terminology to everyday life and experi-ence. There is a danger that such an exercise may lead to the excessive reference to Hebrew and Greek roots every time we speak. This becomes boring for our audiences and, in fact, can become a bondage for the speaker. If this happens it is more likely to alienate our congregation rather than communicate with them because they may be left with an impression of our own learning rather than a revelation of the word of God.

There are other Bible helps which rank alongside concord-ances. Recently I was presented with a superb thirteen volume series called *The Complete Biblical Library*, a com-prehensive Bible study system first devised by a Norwegian pastor and now produced in the United States. It is a terrific introduction to the text of the New Testament with six volumes of Greek Lexicon. Again, it is not essential to be a Greek student to get the benefit of all this. The information is readily accessible to every believer with a modicum of intelligence.

Thirdly, other background reading

This next area of our preparation for study concerns the books we can read to set the scene, as it were, for the Scriptures. Anybody who wants to make sense of the Scriptures in a real way must engage in some background reading. It is not a matter of us being theologians to do this as there are many tremendous helps on the market. I suggest that our background reading should have three main aspects to it:

(1) *Historical.* This sort of reading provides a context for our understanding of the Scriptures. The Bible is not unrelated to the events of history and it is going to greatly enhance our appreciation of the message of the Scriptures if we can see how these historical events relate to each other. Questions of culture and background help us to distinguish that which is time-conditioned from that which is relevant in every generation. Habits and customs often help us to see into the deeper significance of an act or a statement, which otherwise, we might misunderstand or misapply.

There are many useful helps on the market in this area. At a popular level the Lion publications provide a number of interesting and helpful handbooks. There are, of course, innumerable specialist books dealing with specific sections of history and the Scriptures. All of these will be helpful to our greater appreciation and understanding of Old and New Testaments alike.

(2) *Exegetical.* This simply means bringing the meaning and significance from the text. To this end there are again a whole number of books that will help. Some of the introductory series of commentaries will prove useful here and will both clarify and control our own interpretation of Scripture.

(3) *Theological.* As I have said before, one of the reasons that many people are not so confident about speaking in public, lies in the fact that they suffer a lack of clarity about what they really believe. I would commend a clear and straightforward Introduction to Theology. This may immediately distance some readers from my advice so far but we need to understand that I am not suggesting some obscure, lifeless tome that is of use only to some esoteric specialists. No, I would suggest an Introduction such as *Introducing Christian Doctrine* by Millard Erikson (published by Baker Bookhouse, Grand Rapids Michigan).

Theology helps us to understand the major themes of the faith and see how they come from and relate to the Scriptures, e.g. redemption, salvation and so on. Dr J. Rodman Williams of Regent University has published a three volume work called *Renewal Theology* which I would commend especially to those who want to understand the subject from a sympathetic charismatic point of view. These books are most readable and will reward any reader who cares to give some time and application to their study.

These types of books are worth their weight in gold in terms of the back-up to your Scripture reading and essential if you want to be a communicating preacher/teacher.

(c) The question of the relationship between preaching and the Scriptures

Of course, there are some who would not see any necessary connection between preaching and the Bible. They would put such a stress on the present dimension of the word that they might not see any need for it to be connected in a direct way with the words of Scripture. This may be particularly true of those who see themselves involved in prophetic preaching.

I have no doubt that it is perfectly possible to give a word inspired by the Holy Spirit which speaks directly to the current situation without any direct allusion to or exegesis of the Scriptures. Indeed, I would lay claim to having been involved in this sort of proclamation myself.

However, such exercises must stay very close to the spirit of Scripture and if the Body of Christ ever found its diet of preaching consisting only of such prophetic words then it would be exposed to two dangers. First, the danger of failing to enjoy the richness of a full diet of style, presentation and method. Second, the danger of being led astray into the realm of human ideas and delusion that finds itself at odds with the revelation of the Scriptures.

A close relationship with the Scriptures in our preaching and teaching and, indeed, in our prophetic ministry, will provide not only a stimulus to our spirits but a necessary control to save the church from heresy.

In particular, I have found a simple diagram like the one below helpful in maintaining an appreciation of how my preaching may relate to Scripture in a variety of different ways. It would be fair to say that the purpose and style of what we want to say will determine or be determined by our relation to Scripture.

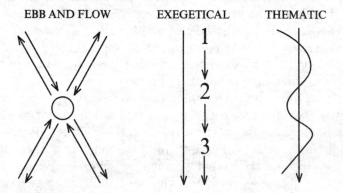

EBB AND FLOW   EXEGETICAL   THEMATIC

These **three simple images** describe for us the different movements relative to Scripture in preaching and teaching.

The first image, I've described as **ebb and flow**. For example, if we are giving a word of exhortation or involved in devotional teaching, it's likely that there will be one central biblical idea that we may ebb and flow towards and away from. We will use an illustration, a scripture, a personal experience and move in and out, but all the time we'll keep coming back to the same idea. Because that will be what God wants to say.

On the other hand, **an exegetical address** will have a style that goes from A to Z. We won't go in and out of the text, but will live with it. What we are doing is bringing meaning out of the text, we are expounding something – the style is different from above and perhaps more coherent.

Finally, we come to what I describe as **the thematic style**. Here there is one theme that runs throughout and the examples from Scripture interweave with this. For example, the central theme may be faith. We may start with Abraham as a great Old Testament example of faith, come through the prophets and end up somewhere in the New Testament.

These simple diagrams are practical visual helps to enable our understanding of how to communicate. The most essential thing of all, of course, is that we have some clear idea of what we are aiming at when we speak.

I remember seeing an advertisement for the Motor Show in London. It showed three cars cobbled together; the nose of a saloon car, the middle of another car and the back end of a racing car. The point of the ad was that if you didn't know one end of a car from another, you should go to the Motor Show then you'd get to know.

If we are going to communicate effectively, then we must know the difference between one thing and another and what tools are available to help us do the job more effectively. Only in this way will we ever fulfil the injunction of the text with which we began that we might present ourselves to God without shame as workmen who have applied themselves to their calling and who know how to effectively handle the word with which we are entrusted.

Chapter 8

Into Action

In the last chapter we looked at what we should be doing to prepare ourselves to share the word. Let's now take a look at the action itself. There are two major areas we need to consider when we want to communicate anything in public. The first, although not in order of precedence, is the state of the audience. Many people either cannot or do not want to listen in depth. In relation to Christian truth Paul warned that *'the time will come when men will not put up with sound doctrine'* (2 Timothy 4:3) and this may be a challenge we face in our own day. The second has more to do with ourselves as communicators. Are we always breaking up the bread of life in such a way that enables people to get a hold of it? The late Harry Truman, one time President of the United States, is reputed to have had a little sign on his desk which read 'The buck stops here'. This may seem a very unbiblical or untheological illustration to use but it is essential for every preacher or teacher to understand the need to take responsibility for their actions in ministry. We can blame everyone else – the audience, the congregation, whoever – but surely as far as preparation goes and how we carry out the task it is true that 'the buck stops here'.

In this chapter we will look at some simple principles which will help us to develop practical skills that will enhance our communicative abilities.

1. Getting it Together

Novices usually commit a number of crimes with relation to communication.

First, they often put too much into one address. For the sake of interest, impact, clarity and the proper development of skills we should start simply and with an economy of time and words. Skills develop with practice. Clarity of ideas and speech, pronunciation, communication; all should improve with progress. Don't start too fussy. This sin leads to too many ideas competing at once for people's imagination or memory. Their brain will become overcrowded and they will be in danger of going into information shock.

People sometimes ask me whether they should use notes when they are speaking. It is, in the end, not really a question about whether to have notes or not but rather a question of proper preparation. No communicator should be slavishly tied to notes. Notes are a useful memory aid but the subject should have already found its place in mind and spirit so that it comes out with freshness and a personal touch. If it is lodged in the mind it will come out with clarity; if it is in the spirit it will come out with life and power. Of course one thing which is worse than too many notes is the person who says that they rely totally on the Holy Spirit's leading. Perhaps this novice has seen a great speaker who seemed to be able to communicate so fluently without relying on any outward help. The novice tries to copy the mentor but with results that are very different! The truth is that we all find help and security from some sort of outline, simple or otherwise. Speaking for myself I find that the occasion determines what sort of notes I need.

If it is the sort of meeting where spontaneity and vitality are to be key features then I try to ensure that such notes as I use, do not impede the free flow of the Spirit. If, on the other hand, precision and close argument are required it is more likely that I would use fairly full notes to guide my thoughts.

One thing needs to be made crystal clear and it is the fact that the Holy Spirit is not bound because you use notes. In some circles it used to be frowned upon if the speaker resorted to notes. That speaker was regarded as unspiritual and not truly led by the Holy Spirit. The evidence of such an attitude is all too clear and sad to see in fellowships which have increasingly become irrelevant to the needs of their day.

2. From Beginning to End

There are three main elements in any decent speech, talk or sermon – the beginning, the middle (the body) and the end. In other words: we need to know how to start, how to continue and how to finish. A well known axiom of communication is contained in the phrase; 'he who begins well, ends well'.

The beginning

Charles Spurgeon, who was one of the greatest Christian preachers ever, gave the following advice to his students:

> 'Gentlemen – don't go creeping into your subject as some swimmers go into the water; first to the ankles and then to the knees and then to the waist and shoulders. Plunge into it at once, over the head and shoulders.' [1]

Spurgeon was right, in the main – we should establish with our audience as soon as possible the essence of what we mean to talk about. However, there are some things that we have to deal with in our modern context which Spurgeon never had to contend with to the same degree. One can only guess, but preaching to twenty thousand people in the Metropolitan Tabernacle during last century was probably different from communicating to one hundred and twenty (including highly mobile children) in the context of a school classroom (which passes as the church building), as is often the case today! So apart from the fact that we have got the right opening in mind and have thought of our best opening gambit there may be other factors which affect the beginning.

The question of context

Preaching takes place within a context. By this I don't mean the place or the atmosphere or even the people. These are all subjects we have dealt with elsewhere. I am speaking of the fact that our preaching usually happens in connection with other spiritual events like praise and worship. It may be that the context produced by what has happened before is not conducive to our launching straight in to our subject without some other action. It is rare today that the speaker will be in control of the meeting from the outset. Then it would be possible to ensure that what precedes the word is suitable to what is going to be shared and to how we want to say it. The mood created by the elements of the service prior to the word being spoken may be entirely different from the mood of the word. Or it may be that what has come before has been nothing short of disastrous. The effect of what has gone before may have created a situation in which the mood and expectations of the people are in direct contradiction to the spirit of the word which is about to be shared. The secret is to learn how to build bridges between what has happened and what is about to happen through the preaching.

Anyone who seriously intends to be an effective communicator needs to learn to regard the context and never take it for granted. One important lesson to be learnt is how to guard the word that is in the heart whatever happens around it. A second lesson is to know how to turn any situation, if necessary, so that what has already happened becomes a help and not a hindrance to what is to be said. There are many ways by which this may be achieved. Something as straightforward as the introduction of a simple, suitable song before the talk can change the whole atmosphere. Or again it may be helpful to talk about some introductory subject for a few moments without detracting from the main body of what is to be said. For example, I sometimes find it appropriate to introduce one of my books or speak for a moment about some aspect of wider ministry or some such topic. This can serve a number of functions apart from changing the atmosphere such as giving the audience an opportunity to tune in to a new voice or accent or prepare their minds and concentration on what is about to be said.

Experience teaches one the different ways in which the gap between what has already happened and what we now have to say may be bridged effectively. The most important lesson to learn is that every occasion will be different and different needs demand different answers. **Let me illustrate what I mean by the use of three words**.

The first is **appeasement**. This may seem a very strange word to use with regard to communicating something so wonderful and loving as the gospel. However, you can imagine an occasion when all that has happened before is all right in itself but not quite appropriate as a setting for the word to be shared. In this case it may be the thing to do to 'make friends' with the preceding events in a spiritually connective way. It is sometimes important to connect oneself purposefully with what has happened, through humour or some remarks. This has the effect of making the flow seem to carry on, whether or not it really did. This is the principle of appeasement. The audience is not aware of it, of course – it's something that is learnt through experience and sensitivity of spirit.

The second word is **contrast**. There are times, of course, when it will be impossible to follow the principle outlined above. Then you have to recognise the situation and do something that radically changes the mood. It is possible to begin your presentation or address as though it was something completely new. I have often found, in fact, that this is not a hindrance but a help because it can be used to contrast the message one wants to share with everything else and make it be seen in the best possible light. This might especially be the case if you perceive that the audience or congregation shares your own feelings on the preceding events. It is important, if possible, that such a contrasting approach be taken without crushing or demeaning anyone else involved in the occasion up to that point. Nevertheless, it would be true to say that there have been times when I have just had to make it clear that what is coming is totally different in nature and content to what has just happened even at the risk of hurting someone's feelings.

This leads to the third word, **confrontation**. Sometimes it is impossible to take a more diplomatic path and the situation has to be confronted. I have certainly been in meetings where I've had to apologise and make it clear that what has been laid on my heart was completely different to what had already happened. This isn't easy and there are no set words, but it's essential that we are honest if we are going to bring God's word in the way He intends it to be brought.

Continuing with the action

Now we are in the middle of the action, we are addressing the people in our preaching or teaching. This is a good time to take stock of some basic principles we have expanded on elsewhere. **Here are five simple but important points**.

(a) **Know what you want to say** – the content ... the mood ... the shape ... the aim. If the preparation has been done properly, these things will unfold. Preparation isn't only about putting words or outlines on paper, it's a preparation of heart and spirit. Christian communicators don't just come at people over a sheet of paper! The construct may be on the paper, but the mood, the aim and the clarity are in our hearts. If we are prepared properly in heart and in the physical, when it comes to the actual doing of the job, we will be sharing out of what is a reality within us. Really good preaching or teaching is a spiritual replay on a larger screen of what has already been played on the individual screen of your life.

(b) **Audience involvement** – You need to capture your audience! Never imagine they are already captivated when you stand up. It's your job to win them, to capture their attention, to grip their hearts. We need to get ourselves involved with our audience. Although our communication may be a monologue as far as vocal sound is concerned, it should never be a spiritual monologue. There must be a reaching inside of people, the establishment of an inward dialogue.

(c) **Emphasis and clarity** – It is important to know what parts of the address need special clarity or emphasis and what the highlights are. It is generally accepted that people only retain about ten per cent of what they hear and that only for a time. So it's important that this ten per cent contains the essence of the message we want to get across. The highlights need to be in that ten per cent. Perhaps they will remember an illustration, but that illustration should draw through into memory the recollection of the main point. Illustration is a very useful tool in effective communication but illustration just for its own sake is meaningless. It needs to be a memory aid to the main point of the message.

The fact that most people can't remember what they've heard is perhaps a judgement on the standard of spiritual communication today. Each of us needs to be our own worst critic. Is that favourite story you use just a filler? Is it waffle? If it is, cut it out. Only use an illustration that will pull the point through. In that way if a listener remembers the illustration they have a chance of remembering the point of it.

(d) **Light and shade** – Having established the main points of emphasis, we now need some light and shade. One criticism I make sometimes of speakers I hear is that they rarely seem to vary their voice. They neither vary the tone nor the speed or the mood. Everything is either sober or a running joke. Yet one of the most powerful ways of communicating is to have people coming right to the edge of the cliff with hilarity, then suddenly to drop them into the depths of a profoundly serious and thought provoking point. The effect is not only dramatic, it can be the most powerfully challenging and life changing way of speaking into their experience. Remembering the ten per cent retention factor, the use of light and shade is also a good way of re-emphasizing the main points of the address. One time you can say them with humour, another time in complete seriousness.

(e) **There must be repetition** – people do not tend to remember what they are told only once. We Christian preachers sometimes fall into the sin of assuming certain things about the people we're speaking to. We assume they read as many books as we do, that they know as many words as we do, that they can envision in their brain those great theological ideas we have on paper. The truth is that they don't and they can't. So we must repeat and repeat in such a way – with clarity, emphasis and variety – that people will remember.

If you want to communicate effectively you need to practise the inward art of objectivity to your content. Of course we're passionately involved. The gospel is our gospel, we've experienced the subject, so there's emotion involved. Somehow, though, we need to be able to stand back and look at ourselves as we're preaching. This doesn't happen at first because we tend to be caught up with the challenge and excitement of the moment. It is an ability that needs to grow with time and experience. It does help, however, if we can develop a proper self-consciousness while we are speaking. It helps if we can be conscious of the ups and downs, the lights and shades, the emphases and the effects. Personally speaking, I find that this is what gives preaching a very profound level of satisfaction. If you don't enjoy your word, there's little chance of anyone else enjoying it. If you don't feel the power of sin, the power of conviction, the depth of the awesomeness of God, the power of the holiness of God and respond within yourself, then there's no chance of anyone else doing it. When you finish you should know where you've taken the people, because this should be the second time at least that you've gone there; once in the preparation, now in the presentation. If you don't go there you will never take anybody else with you.

Words

Watchman Nee put it so well when he said,

> 'You must learn to speak until people can comprehend
> you from the moment you begin. Do not speak for half
> an hour when people only understood five minutes of it
> – it is better to speak less than waste twenty-five
> minutes.'[2]

Words are not an end in themselves, but the power line of
our communication. When we use words we're throwing out
a line. One end connects with the speaker, the other with the
listener. Power needs to come down this line and this is
where the words we use are so important. It's like laying an
electric cable: if you need a particular density of power you
must be sure to lay the right style of cable otherwise it won't
be able to carry the power. Our words affect whether or not
the power of our communication comes through. It is important that we learn to listen to ourselves and ask if we really
mean what we are saying or if we need to say it like that. We
need to recognize what impression is being left in the minds
of other people by the way we use words and by what words
we say.

There are certain questions in particular we might address
ourselves to if we are to improve the effectiveness of our
communication.

(a) The question of relevance

It is important to enquire about the relevance of the language we use. Are our words relevant to those we are
addressing? We may be guilty of using outdated language in
our preaching and teaching, especially if we stick too closely
to the text of the Authorised Version of the Bible. The days
have long since passed when all school children were taught
from these Scriptures. This is not only true outside the
fellowship of Christian believers, but it is also the case
inside. Many, many people will never have come across
words the way they are used in older translations of the

Bible and they can be quite confused by them. Take, for example, the phrase 'without let or hindrance'. Maybe a lawyer would understand the phrase but what might it mean to a young person listening? The old word 'let' is equivalent to 'prevent' in modern speech so it is confusing to a modern ear where the word means 'to permit', the very opposite of its intention in the King James Version. Another example is the word, 'without'; 'Jesus was without the city'. Now when someone reads the passage where this comes, they can probably see from the context that it doesn't mean that Jesus hadn't got a city, but listening to something is a different matter from reading the text. The word 'without' means simply outside. For a listener one strange word without explanation can destroy concentration for everything else. Language changes and it's our job, as communicators, to employ words that make sense to the hearers of our own generation.

Of course, it is not simply a question of archaic language being the problem. Words from one context take on a completely different meaning in another and if we are not careful people can be completely confused. For example, there are some technical terms in use today that can throw unsuspecting victims into complete confusion. The prime example of this is in the world of computer jargon. Who would ever have thought that a 'mouse' was ever anything other than a cheese-nibbling rodent. When I was asked if I wanted a 'mouse' with my computer, I wondered what they were talking about! Then I was shown that it was a useful little tool by which I could control the operation of the screen – nothing to do with tails and cheeses! Another one is a 'bus'. Surely, a large vehicle with around six wheels specially made to carry passengers? Nothing to do with that – it's a power distribution system that determines the capacity of my computer in terms of memory storage. It distributes electricity, power and memory. Language changes a preacher's job. The way it is rapidly transposing itself from one context to another is a challenge we all have to face.

(b) The question of redundancy

Of all communicators I think that preachers are the most guilty of using redundant words. In a nutshell, redundant words are words that don't need to be there at all, they are space-fillers. One thing I get upset about, especially when I find myself doing it, is the misuse of the word 'just'. This is a very common occurrence amongst Christians today particularly in the realm of public praying. We tell the Lord that we 'just' want this and we 'just' want that. I don't know where the habit has come from but it is quite out of keeping with the idea that we can come before the throne of grace with confidence.

Even great words like 'hallelujah' and its more modern equivalent 'praise the Lord' can become redundant words. In certain traditions they have become mere words of emphasis that the speaker will use when he wants to underline a point, or take a breath or sometimes it sounds like he's not quite sure what to say next. Injecting a couple of 'hallelujahs' and 'praise the Lord' might seem to give some sort of spiritual credibility to what otherwise might have been a fairly thin theological argument! Did the speaker really mean 'hallelujah'? Was the name of the Lord really lifted up? Or was it just a slogan? This is one area where much more discipline is needed.

(c) The question of recovery

For the communicator this is, I believe, an area of great interest and challenge. Someone once said, 'Recover a word and discover a universe.'

There are some words and biblical terms that some people would want to jettison, but they're perfectly acceptable if the preacher does his job properly. Just because a word is unfamiliar outside of the Christian sphere is insufficient reason to want to exclude it from the domain of the Christian communicator. We want to be rid of words used to no effect, or words that are irrelevant, but when it comes to technical words, names, words of theological power, that is something different. Here lies the heart of the challenge to the real preacher. Can he use these words in such a way as to bring people rapidly into an understanding of the essence of them, and from that lead them into a new area of understanding and, perhaps, experience?

Take, for example, great words like 'justification', 'redemption', 'holiness' and so on. These, and many others, are all words that are outside the normal framework of everyday language. Yet, they are the technical words of our trade. If I go to a computer analyst, or a financial expert, they will use words in relation to their subject which are outside my normal terms of reference and they can only make them meaningful to me if they transpose them into terms which I can understand. At the same time, these are the terms of their expertise. So they don't discard them, they explain them. We must not be ashamed of the fact that there are specialist ideas and terms which relate to our faith. Our job is to communicate those ideas in such a way that gives our listeners a real entrance into the heartland of what the terms mean. Otherwise we will have to strip from the Bible every word and phrase which is otherwise unintelligible to the human ear. We might discover that we have little left.

An example of this was brought home to me powerfully when I first bought a copy of the New International Version of the Scriptures. One of the first things I noticed is that they had chosen to alter the Old Testament phrase, 'the Lord of Hosts', because, they say, it isn't a meaningful term to the modern reader. They have substituted the title 'Lord Almighty' everywhere the name 'Lord of Hosts' occurs. Now in Hebrew and in English, these are two completely different terms, both in function and in meaning and we deprive people of so much wealth when we change things like this. The saying I quoted earlier about recovering a word and discovering a universe comes into play in a case like this. Rather than discard the title we are presented with a fantastic opportunity to communicate its real meaning to our hearers. When we are really communicating colourfully, using Bible illustrations to show what the 'Lord of Hosts' means we can leave people with a fresh grasp of its significance for their own experience. An instance like this seems to me to be a failure of nerve on the part of translators and perhaps a failure on the part of us modern communicators to do the job properly. Let's not get rid of words that are important, but rather learn to interpret them in such a way that people can get to grips with them.

3. The Bottom Line

The ending is just as important as the beginning. This is a principle that is well recognised in business life. The best communication in the world is no communication at all without a bottom line. Every decent communicator needs to know how to bring their audience to the point of action or commitment. Sometimes we speak of concluding the address. We certainly need to know when to stop! Conclusion, however, is a bit of a dull word. It conjures up mental images of what it sounds like; the end, finale. The bottom line of preaching isn't the end at all however, it ought only to be a new beginning. Our ending should have all the ingredients, all the potentiality for somebody else's beginning. Let us recall for a moment what we've been trying to achieve in our spiritual communication.

Real communication has a three-fold aim:

(1) **To illumine people's minds** – The message must have real and clear content.

(2) **To stir people's emotions** – We need to reach inside people if we're to open them up to new truths or ideas. Let me say again that this is not emotionalism through which we are trying to dislocate our hearers from the due and proper processes of judgement and thought. It simply means that we are addressing the whole person, intellectually and spiritually, so the word we speak from God will penetrate right to the inner depths of their being.

(3) **To activate their wills** – People must be brought to a point of choice or action. If the message is clear and

effective it will lead to a question such as 'What do I do now?'

Peter's address on the day of Pentecost, which is recorded in the second chapter of the book of Acts, contains these very elements. And it all ended with the question *'What shall we do?'*

The conclusion needs to perform certain important functions

– **It should show people where they've arrived at.** There should be no doubt about the ending. It should gather up in itself the essence of all that's been said. This can mean giving a brief resumé, but usually we should end in such a way that the heart of the message stands up for all to see.

– **It should contain an element of definite ending.** Sometimes this will involve a sense of heightening or crisis. The great Scots preacher, James Stewart, used to advise his students never to end like that. He always ended quietly and reflectively. This was possibly a reaction to a tradition which marked a previous era in which rhetoric and poetic coloration had been used to add a sense of drama and crisis to the address and which had, in the process, become false and stale. There is no law of homiletics which says how an ending must be. The point is that it has to be the right ending. Here we need to be open to the Holy Spirit's leading every time we preach.

– **It should lead to appropriate action on the part of the people.** Whether there is to be a time of ministry or whether it leads to a time of reflection when the people go away and let the word of God *'dwell in them richly'*, the ending must contribute to what the following action is. It is important how we finish, but it is just as important that we finish. If need be let the ending be clinical and leave the point in people's minds so that they can really grasp the word of God. It is the word of God they need and so it is the word of God we must leave with them.

> *'So is my word that goes out from my mouth: It will not return to me empty, but will accomplish what I desire and achieve the purpose for which I sent it.'* (Isaiah 55:11)

This is what the word of God is sent forth to do, this is the chief purpose of all our spiritual communication.

References

1. Spurgeon, C.H. 1954. *Lectures to My Students on the Art of Preaching*. Marshall Morgan Scott
2. Nee, Watchman. 1971. *The Ministry of God's Word*. Christian Fellowship Publishers Inc.

Chapter 9

The Flow of the Spirit

'God anoints men, not machines.'   (E.M. Bounds)

Someone sent me a cutting from a Christian magazine recently. It was a brief article by an American Pentecostal pastor on the subject of preaching. It started like this:

'Preaching is the consecration of great thoughts carried on the wings of and with all the force and power of an eternal soul. It is God's gift to mankind. It is the ability to think out loud without succession of thought, the ability to think on your feet. It is the gift of continuous impartation of thoughts. It is the faculty of mental arousal and stimulation of the soul and spirit. Preaching is the anointed teaching of God's word.' [1]

It was these very last words which caught my eye. The word anointing is not actually used in the New Testament in the way that we popularly employ it today. When we speak of anointing we mean much the same thing as our American friend in the quotation above. We think of life and flow, of power and enabling, of spontaneity and clarity. Anointing means the ease of the Holy Spirit.

In the New Testament the word is used of believers in two main contexts. The first is 2 Corinthians 1:21 where Paul speaks of the initial anointing of believers in the Holy Spirit – that initial sealing of the Holy Spirit that testifies to the life of Christ in us. This is the birthright of every believer.

'Now it is God who makes both us and you stand firm in Christ. He anointed us . . . '

The other is in 1 John 2:20:

'You have an anointing from the Holy One, and all of you know the truth.'

Both these Scriptures speak of a work of the Spirit that is fundamental to being a Christian believer. The inward testimony of the Spirit of which Paul also speaks in Romans 8:16 and the revelation of the truth concerning Jesus into our hearts. The same sort of revelation of which Paul speaks in 2 Corinthians 3:16 where he tells us that when a person turns to the Lord through the initiative of the Holy Spirit the veil that was over their minds is taken away.

As long as we understand what we mean, I think it is quite legitimate to use the word anointing in the way which has become popular today. Here we are using the word in a more popular sense to speak of a special enabling of the human spirit by the Spirit of God. In this sense it is very appropriate to our subject of preaching and teaching. In Psalm 133 we hear of the anointing oil which was poured on Aaron's head and which ran down on his beard. This anointing with oil is a vivid physical example of what is true in spiritual anointing. When I think of anointing, I think of something vital and flowing; something of freshness, enabling and power – all desperately needed by the preacher of God's word. This is the sort of anointing we must desire from our hearts. How can we preach unless we're enabled by the greatest communicator that Jesus ever sent on the earth – the Holy Spirit?

Jesus said:

'When He, the Spirit of truth, has come, He will guide you into all truth; for He will not speak on His own authority . . . He will take of what is Mine and declare it to you.'　　　　　　　　　　　　　　　(John 16:13, 14 NKJ)

We need the divine declarer in our hearts – that's what I mean by anointing.

Some of the greatest preachers in history have testified personally to the difference this on-coming of the Holy Spirit made in their preaching ministry. Take, for example, the experience of the great American evangelist D.L. Moody. His biographer records a profound experience which Moody went through at a critical stage of his ministry. It was October 1871 the year of the great fire of Chicago. Moody was experiencing a period of spiritual turmoil and unrest. The record tells it like this:

'At the close of the service two women whom he had frequently noticed in attendance came forward and said they were praying for him, as they felt he needed "the power of the Spirit". "I need the power! Why," said he in telling of the interview, "I thought I had the power! I had the largest congregation in Chicago, and there were many conversions. I was in a sense satisfied. But right along these two godly women kept praying for me, and their earnest talk about 'anointing for special service' set me thinking. I asked them to come and talk with me, and they poured out their hearts in prayer that I might receive the filling of the Holy Spirit. There came a great hunger into my soul. I did not know what it was. I began to cry out as I had never done before. I really felt that I did not want to live if I could not have this power for service."'

He continues:

'"My heart was not in the work of begging. I could not appeal. I was crying out all the time that God would fill me with His Spirit. Well, one day in the city of New York – oh what a day! – I cannot describe it, I seldom refer to it; it is almost too sacred an experience to name. Paul had an experience of which he never spoke for fourteen years. I can only say that God revealed

Himself to me, I had such an experience of His love that I had to ask Him to stay His hand. I went to preaching again. The sermons were not different; I did not present any new truths, and yet hundreds were converted. I would not now be placed back where I was before that blessed experience if you would give me all the world – it would be as small as dust in the balance." '[2]

Someone else once commenting on this testimony said: 'The sermons were not different, but the servant was!'

The anointing of God in our ministry makes such a difference. It brings a release of the spirit. Jesus said that whoever believed in Him would find streams of living water flowing from within him (John 7:38). The anointing of the Holy Spirit has this effect. It brings a release of power. This was the promise of the risen Jesus to his disciples.

> *'You will receive power when the Holy Spirit comes upon you.'* (Acts 1:8)

It brings a release of life. Paul draws a contrast between the limited capacity of man in his sin and fallen humanity who takes his lineage from the first Adam and the spiritual life that is released through Jesus.

> *'So it is written: "The first man Adam became a living being"; the last Adam, a life-giving spirit.'* (1 Corinthians 15:45)

It brings a release of light.

> *'For God who said, "Let light shine out of darkness" made his light shine in our hearts to give us the light of the knowledge of the glory of God.'* (2 Corinthians 4:6)

Kenneth Hagin somewhere identifies three significant factors which affect the anointing of God in our lives and ministry. He describes them as association, environment and influence. To a large degree I think he is right. Those of us with any experience in the ways of God understand those things which enable our spirits and open them to the flow of God's Spirit. Equally we know well those factors which inhibit our spirits and prevent the Holy Spirit from flowing freely through us. The Old Testament witnesses on a number of occasions to the reality of these things.

We recall, for example, the experience of Elisha the prophet recorded in 2 Kings 3:15ff. The prophet calls for a harpist. Music is so often used by God to stimulate the spirit of man.

> 'While the harpist was playing, the hand of the Lord came upon Elisha and he said, "This is what the Lord says..."'

If we want to know what anointing is and how to share in it we need to put ourselves in line with those people and places where the anointing operates.

The Effect of the Anointing

I can identify a variety of effects when the anointing of God moves upon my spirit.

First, it brings a stirring in the spirit

It is as though something becomes alive inside your spirit. I don't think it is an accident that so many of the sensations of the presence of the anointing are almost physical. There is a very profound link between the inner and outer man and when God's Spirit begins to move the effect inside is tangible. When the anointing of God is present there is a deep inner movement of spirit.

Second, it brings a sense of refreshment of soul and body

I often find that the sheer demands of life and ministry take their toll on my body and some days I ache with tiredness in my arms and legs. When, however, the anointing of God comes the tiredness and weariness of body and soul disappears! The anointing of God is a life-giving thing and gives refreshment to spirit, soul and body. I have sometimes started a meeting feeling like death warmed up but when the anointing began to flow with the word I have found myself the first beneficiary of the movement of God's Spirit.

Third, it brings an encouragement of heart

The anointing of God is uplifting to the heart. If the preacher gets uplifted, there's a good chance that the congregation will as well. Maybe some of the depression in congregations is because of preachers trying to fulfil their calling without the anointing of God.

Fourth, it brings deepened understanding and insight

A message cannot properly be prepared only in an analytical and rational manner. Revelation transcends reason. That does not mean that our thought processes are unimportant and that our research is in vain. It does, however, recognize that the anointing of God is more than the sum total of all our study and reason. As we will see later, one important feature of revelation is that it is in essence a breakthrough from God. An anointed preacher experiences a flowing through his mind as God quickens his understanding in the Holy Spirit. Things become clear that otherwise never would be.

Fifth, it brings an increased clarity of thought and vision

When I'm living in the anointing of the Holy Spirit, I've found that my memory gets so clear, I can retain things and recall things. I get a very clear vision of what I've got to say and do. One of the real challenges in preaching is to show that you know where you're going, where you've come from and what you're aiming at. If the preacher isn't clear, the people never will be. *'If the trumpet makes an uncertain sound, who will prepare for battle?'* A preacher should have acid clarity about what he's saying. Why? Because he should already have received the message himself from God.

Preaching isn't a guessing game, it's a delivery of something received.

Sixth, it brings a fresh flow of spiritual power
Paul says,

> *'My message and my preaching were not with wise and persuasive words, but with a demonstration of the Spirit's power.'* (1 Corinthians 2:4)

Today there's a danger that we only identify power with certain styles of ministry. With the anointing of God there is, however, vital power in the preached word itself. We need to learn once again to let the word have its power rather than substituting something else. The ministry of the word is the prime ministry. Once that is established, then God will direct us beyond that to anything else that is needed. It's the anointing of God that brings the power.

> *'Say the word and my servant will be healed.'*
> (Luke 7:7)

Seventh, it brings a new boldness in spirit
This was the outcome of the coming of the Spirit at Pentecost. The book of Acts rings with this affirmation:

> *'They were all filled with the Holy Spirit and spoke the word of God boldly.'* (Acts 4:31)

Anointing from God brings boldness – *'parrhesia'*. That's a great word in the New Testament. It means unreserved utterance, frankness, candour, cheerful courage. It denotes a divine enabling that comes to ordinary and unprofessional people exhibiting spiritual power and authority. In Acts, the Apostles were channels out of whom the word of God flowed with clarity. I can remember some occasions in my life, being gripped by men who spoke like this and they are occasions that I'll never forget.

Eighth, it brings a heightened sense of the presence of God
When Paul speaks to the Corinthians he tells them to desire the gifts of the Holy Spirit, because as they are displayed then men will *'report that God is truly among you.'* The reality of God's presence in our ministry is surely something to be prized above everything else!

Enabling the Anointing

I came across an illustration of the operation of the anointing in our lives in a most unusual setting. It was at an air show where a new type of helicopter was being demonstrated. This helicopter is known as a Notar because it does not operate by using a rotor blade at the rear end of the boom as in a more traditional model. On a traditional helicopter the most important blade is probably this small rotor blade at the back because it gives the helicopter stability and direction. If this little blade fails it can spell disaster. Research work has been going on for years to overcome this danger. Now it seems they've come up with an answer in this machine that has a tail but no rotor blade. The tail boom is hollow and so acts like a tunnel. The power of an internal fan, driven by the main engine, forces air down through this tunnel and out of a small two millimetre wide slot which runs the length of the boom on one side. The air exits the slot at speeds of up to two hundred miles per hour. The amazing thing is that instead of just exploding out and away from the tail boom, the air hugs the shape of the boom and flows round it. On the opposite side of the boom from the slot out of which the air rushes is a deflection strip which then forces the air away from the boom. The effect of all this is to create a cushion of air on the underside of the boom which gives lift and directive buoyancy to the helicopter. It's amazing!

How is this relevant to what we are saying about the anointing of the Spirit? Well, the fact is that the anointing too follows the shape, in this case the shape of our lives. If conditions are right the anointing will flow and create the buoyancy of God's power in our ministry with great effect. So it's absolutely vital that our shape is God's shape. Our lives need to be in shape, the word we preach needs to be in shape. That's why we need to make sure that it's the truth of God we're preaching, because the anointing follows God's shape.

Inhibiting the Anointing

Just as we have recognized that we can enable the anointing of God by having our minds and lives in the right shape so we need to recognize that there are many factors which have the opposite effect. In other words there are certain factors which inhibit the flow of God's Spirit in our ministry. Sometimes it may be something very simple; at others something deeper in our lives that really needs to be dealt with before we can know the liberty of God in our service.

Let me look at just a few of the most common inhibitors of the anointing.

(a) The burden of other things

I have discovered that if one's heart is burdened or exercised about needs or other cares this can stifle the anointing of God in one's spirit. For example, it may be concern at the financial level. I know in my own experience how much I have had to rely on God to take away the extra burden of care and anxiety that can come at this level. If not money then it may be a burden about people. Perhaps the people you are responsible for in the Lord. I have tried to learn (but still have a long way to go) to do what the Scriptures say at a practical level. That is, to cast my burden on the Lord that He might sustain me. I have frequently found it necessary to carry this process out within my imagination, to picture how I feel and the area of my concern and consciously to do a spiritual transfer between myself and God. My reasoning in a moment like this is simple. It is God's work after all and if He wants to see it accomplished He will need to carry the load. Invariably I have found that He has a stronger arm than I have.

(b) Fear of circumstances or situations

Sometimes it is merely the fact that you find yourself on unfamiliar ground. Or perhaps it's the people who are different. The fear of man says the Scriptures, brings a snare. This is no more true than for the preacher or communicator who can be greatly affected in spirit by the place or the people. I recall one occasion at least where my liberty of spirit was greatly affected for a time by the presence of a person in the congregation who I did not expect to see there. It was a temporary disablement but enough to remind me of the power of places and people with whom we are either unfamiliar or taken by surprise.

(c) Self-consciousness

Many, many years ago I was asked to preach in the Sunday evening service of the brethren assembly where my wife's family were members. My dear mother-in-law was very proud of the fact that her new prospective son-in-law had been asked to take the prime spot so to speak. I made two drastic mistakes. Firstly, I wore a new suit. The suit had never been worn before. In fact it had only been delivered from the tailors the previous day. I have always taught my students that it is better never to preach or speak in public on the first wearing of new clothes. No one else may know or notice but it does create a self-conscious spirit.

The second mistake I made was to compound the felony by giving in to one other demand. My dear mother-in-law thought I should have a handkerchief in my top pocket to complete the effect. This is something I never normally do so you can imagine how much it added to all the feelings of self-consciousness. All of this, added to a feeling of extreme vulnerability in the presence of so many godly saints and elders, meant that the Holy Spirit had not much chance of breaking through in anointed power.

(d) A striving spirit

Sometimes when we stand up to speak, we get caught up in a desire to impress somebody. None of us are free from the inclination to pride or to the equally insidious tendency to compare ourselves with other speakers or ministers. Instead of flowing in the liberty of the Spirit of God we find instead that we are caught up in an inward struggle.

(e) Fear of past actions or sins

The devil is a past master at bringing feelings of guilt and self-condemnation to the surface. Hidden feelings of unworthiness that can cripple suddenly break through with awesome power and stop the free flow of the Spirit from God. This can be particularly true if you are called to speak on some topic which touches an area of past sin or weakness in your own experience. Some people become totally disabled in preaching, because in their pre-Christian life – or since – they've engaged in some active sin in the area about which they are now going to speak. Of course, that sin may be dead and gone long ago from a practical point of view but the memory of it overwhelms the reality of God's anointing. If this happens, we need to ask for grace to recognize where the feeling comes from and rise up with the help of God's Spirit against it – it is not of God. On the contrary, it is God's plan to use you to speak of that situation to His glory and to the release of others bound by the same sin.

(f) Actual present sin

The debilitating memory of past sin does not arise from the work of the Holy Spirit. However, where someone is trying to preach or teach the word of God with actual, uncleansed, present sin it is a different matter. The effect of this will be to make the speaker a split personality. Active sin saps spiritual confidence and leads to a loss of spiritual power. This is why the Scriptures tell us to guard our hearts. They are indeed 'the well-spring of life.'

(g) The fear of man

I've already touched on this as a surface reaction to someone, but there are situations where this fear of speaking before certain people can cause extreme reactions. The mouth goes dry as you see someone creeping into the back of a meeting you never expected to be there. Or sometimes it's the nature of the audience that is to be addressed. For example, I've had to speak on theological issues with people sitting in front of me, whom I suspected knew a lot more, at a technical level, than I did. In the end you've just got to give yourself over to the Lord and decide that what He's bringing out of your spirit is going to be life-giving.

(h) Critical or negative spirits

Even Jesus found that He could not do the works of God because of the unbelief that surrounded him. Often the problem is not so much inside ourselves but in the spirits of people around. If the balance is affected by too much that is negative; too much cynicism and unbelief then this will have a great effect on the flow of the anointing. It seems to me that for faith to operate in a context there needs to be a flow back of faith as well as an outflow from the heart of the speaker. If the people have a cynical attitude, it can certainly dampen down the anointing of God in you.

(i) Tiredness or other distractions

It almost seems too obvious to say, but we have weak bodies that don't always hold up too well to the demands put on them. However, God has said that those who wait on Him will renew their strength and soar up. So the answer to this is to lean on the Lord for an infilling of His supernatural strength. And to get a good night's sleep when possible!

(j) Ignorance and unpreparedness

This was a lesson I learned years ago well outside the realm of my preaching life. I have already alluded to the fact that at one time in my career I had the job of presenting new medical preparations to medical practitioners. This was fine normally but there were certain situations that called for a far higher degree of preparedness in the subject than normal. This was, for instance, when one was expected to do a presentation for a team of hospital consultants whose specialist knowledge in the field in question was highly developed. I know from first-hand experience what it feels like to suffer the sense of exposure and vulnerability that a lack of preparation can bring. One cannot be confident about something of which one is almost entirely ignorant. This is a factor we need to pay close attention to in our preaching. Because some of the syndromes we suffer have to do in the first place with our lack of understanding of our subject and the unpreparedness of our spirit for the situation.

We must also consider the power of ignorance in other people, or a lack of respect, or a spirit of unbelief, because people are ignorant of the truth of the word of God. Sadly, this is not only true of out there in the market place. It has become increasingly so within the Body of Christ. As personal knowledge and understanding of the Scriptures has slipped away, so has that deep respect for truth and the revelation of God. The fact is that the people have not been educated in the Holy Spirit. There's no sense of reverence. Unbelief is not just a spirit of faithlessness, it's a lack of expectation, a lack of sensitivity to the context. Someone stands up to do the greatest thing they've ever done in their life – declare the mighty, powerful Word of God – and they're surrounded by people who've got no sense of the occasion; no sense that they should sit with a still spirit and listen to God. These things absolutely detract you from the anointing.

(k) Bad atmosphere

One final factor to consider is the atmosphere of a place. Any preacher or teacher needs to take that into account. It may be that we have gone with a certain expectation to speak in a particular way, but the atmosphere soon betrays the fact that a different approach needs to be adopted. This is where openness to the Holy Spirit is absolutely essential to maintain the anointing of God.

No doubt there are many other factors which could be mentioned that can have a material effect on the anointing in a negative way and I'm sure every preacher could compile their own list. I draw attention to these in particular because I have found them to be areas in which constant care is needed. It will benefit all of us as individuals to pay attention to the things that we have come to recognize as common danger areas in our own experience and continually maintain that openness to the Holy Spirit.

References

1. From 'What is Preaching?' an article by Rev. Nathan Phillips, AEGA ordained minister, Director of Ministerial Affairs for the AEGA Great Texas region, and pastor of Trinity Tabernacle, Pasadena, Texas, USA
2. Edman, V. Redmond. 1984. *They Found the Secret*. Zondervan

Chapter 10

Spirit and Word

It is reported that one week before he died in 1947 Smith Wigglesworth, the enigmatic plumber turned preacher, prophet and healer gave a remarkable prophecy in which he foretold two great moves of the Holy Spirit which would take place after his death. The first move would bring a restoration of the gifts of the Spirit, the second would bring a revival of emphasis on the word of God. He said,

> 'When these two moves of the Spirit combine, we shall see the greatest move the Church of Jesus Christ has ever seen.'[1]

The moment I first read these words my heart leapt because I knew in my own spirit that this word is so relevant to our own times. We have seen the fulfilment of the first part of this prophecy all over the world. A whole new generation of believers have been birthed in the power of God and signs and wonders have testified to God's saving power all round the globe. Now we are to move into the fulfilment of this word as we see a great revival of the living power of the word of God among the nations. However, the word does not operate in a vacuum; it takes men and women to be dedicated to the task, to be vessels ready for the Master's use, to become proclaimers of the word to the ends of the earth.

Piercing and Progressive

Psalm 119:130 is a remarkable little verse of Scripture. It defines the powerful action of God's word as it makes its impact in the life of a human being.

At first glance the King James Version seems almost to contradict the New International Version. The older version translates the Scripture like this:

'The entrance of thy words giveth light.'

While the newer translation says:

'The unfolding of your words gives light.'

It is clear that both speak of the action of the word of God within human experience. The sense of the action in each translation seems somewhat different however. The older version uses the word 'entrance' to describe this action; a word which suggests urgency or breakthrough. There seems to be a sense of drama in the idea of entrance. In one sense it means only an opening but in a deeper sense it carries the idea of suddenness. Perhaps the best illustration of this is the picture of a famous actor or singer making an entrance on stage. They don't creep on without notice. There is, perhaps, a fanfare followed by a sudden lifting of the lights; the curtain goes up and there centre stage is the main character of the moment.

Surely this well describes what often happens through the word of God in the power of the Spirit. A life that has previously been in the dark and a heart that has been closed suddenly is thrown open and flooded with light. How many believers could testify to this sudden entrance of the word in this manner!

The New International uses the idea of 'unfolding' which seems altogether a gentler word. Rather than sudden breakthrough it carries the sense of a teacher standing patiently with a pupil gradually introducing a subject line by line, page by page, chapter by chapter. The light dawns progressively as the pupil is led from one level of truth to another. I am sure it is not difficult for us to recognize once again a valid picture of the activity of the Holy Spirit our divine teacher, leading us into all the truth.

These two words are far from contradictory however. Instead they provide a concise pen portrait of the action of the Word and the Spirit in human experience.

(a) **Firstly**, they present us with **two dynamic images of the word of God**. On the one hand piercing and penetrating (Hebrews 4:12), on the other progressive and upbuilding (Jeremiah 31:33). The action of the word is sometimes like that of the surgeon's lance penetrating and incisive in its intention and powerful in effect. At other times it is more gentle and persuasive, shedding light along the way and step by step leading us into a fuller understanding of the things of God.

(b) **Secondly**, they perfectly describe **the dual action of the Holy Spirit in revelation**. The action of the word described above is, of course, dependent on this action of the Holy Spirit. Piercing powerfully into lives with His holy sword (Ephesians 6:17) while at the same time unfolding the word into our hearts as the divine revealer of truth, the teacher whom Jesus promised (John 16:12–15).

The Holy Spirit operates with these two chief aims within our experience:

(1) **Conviction**. Jesus said that when the Spirit came He would convict the world of guilt in regard to sin, of righteousness and of judgement. The convicting work of the Spirit is closely connected in human experience with a sudden breakthrough of light in our spirit as we come under the power of God and feel sensitive about issues or areas of our lives which have never troubled us in that way before.

(2) **Instruction**. The second thing Jesus said about the coming of the Spirit is that He would lead into all truth. His function would be to take that which finds its source in Jesus and reveal it to us.

This dual role of the Holy Spirit answers two fundamental needs of our Christian experience; one is that we do need this kind of breakthrough from the Lord, the second is that we need continually to be built up in our faith. There is a sort of revival which may be described as crisis revival, where the Holy Spirit deals with us chiefly through the first principle, but there is also the need for progressive revival in which the Spirit of God is applying His renewing power through the continual revelation of the word of God in our lives. One must lead to the other if we are to maintain balance in our Christian experience.

If there is no progression in our lives between the crisis breakthroughs then the next crisis only serves to recover ground lost since the last one. This is how some people live, lurching from one spiritual breakthrough to the next with little evidence of mature growth in their lives. If, however, there is progressive build-up then the next time God breaks through in an urgent sense, we will build positively on what has gone before.

It is very easy to identify crisis, of course, from a spiritual and psychological point of view. We can tell when we have felt a great need in our lives, and have felt the rapid and positive effect of that need being met by God. Progressive revelation, however, by its very nature works in a different way adding a little at a time, effecting change much more gradually. Many people fail to understand the psychology of renewal at this level. They always go for the spectacular and rapid change involved in crisis without perhaps understanding the real value of progressive change. So we can see how important this dual action of the Holy Spirit in revelation is for the well-being and balance of our Christian experience.

(c) **Thirdly**, these two translations of Psalm 119:130 also underline **the essence of divine revelation**. Again we might say that it is both immediate and progressive. Often the word comes as a breakthrough of light piercing the darkness and removing unbelief and fear. More often perhaps it comes line upon line and precept upon precept building blocks of truth into our lives and bringing us to maturity of thought and action (James 1:21).

The word would remain lifeless without the action of the Spirit whilst the action of the Spirit is given content, meaning and purpose by the presence of the word.

Psalm 19 reflects the theme of Psalm 119 in relation to the spiritual power of God's word in human experience. Verses 7 to 11 form links with each other in a beautiful description of the living reality of the revelation of God within a life:

> *'The law of the Lord is perfect,*
> *reviving the soul.*
> *The statutes of the Lord are trustworthy,*
> *making wise the simple.*
> *The precepts of the Lord are right,*
> *giving joy to the heart.*
> *The commands of the Lord are radiant,*
> *giving light to the eyes.*
> *The fear of the Lord is pure,*
> *enduring forever.*
> *The ordinances of the Lord are sure*
> *and altogether righteous.*
> *They are much more precious than gold,*
> *than much pure gold;*
> *they are sweeter than honey,*
> *than honey from the comb.*
> *By them is your servant warned;*
> *in keeping them there is great reward.'*

For the Psalmist there was no question of the word of God being a dead thing. It came to him full of power and life; indeed it was the essential reviving influence of his inner being. It came to him as the word of wisdom. Wisdom here is not something esoteric and theoretical. When the Scripture tells us that the statutes of the Lord make wise the simple, it is showing those who understand it something very important. The 'simple' are a very significant class of people in the Old Testament. They are those who are open to anything.

They are not closed to God and His ways but they might be just as open to other influences. They are very impressionable and easily led. In this sense they have no wisdom. God's word has the power to change all that. It comes with revealing and directing power. It is no mere word of advice, bland in character and open-ended in nature. It carries within it the power of change and the way of life. This is what excites me about a proper view of the word of God. It carries all the personal power of God Himself because it comes in the power of the invisible Spirit who conveys all the vitality and personality of the divine Being into our hearts. The two are inseparable. So the Psalmist goes on. God's word brings all that he needs.

Joy to the heart, light to the eyes, direction to the feet, satisfaction to the inner being, the reward of spirit that is the experience of all who choose to walk in obedience to the revelation of God in their lives.

Now if we transpose all this into the realm of our preaching we will grasp in an instant the excitement and the responsibility of the task. No wonder we are enjoined in Scripture that when we speak we should do it as one speaking the very words of God (1 Peter 4:11).

In 2 Corinthians 3:6 Paul reminds us that

> *'He has made us competent as ministers of a new covenant – not of the letter but of the Spirit; for the letter kills, but the Spirit gives life.'*

We need the Holy Spirit to breathe upon every word we speak and make it alive like that. Then there will be a flowing together of the Spirit and the Word that gives **life**!

Spiritual Dynamics

Certain principles of communication are common to every zone of public speaking whether within the realm of Christian preaching or in the wider secular realm. Some of the principles we have already looked at fall into this category.

How to use notes properly; the importance of posture and presentation; the effective use of the voice; the need for eye contact. These and many more are common to all realms of personal communication. In the realm of the Spirit, however, there are certain factors which are unique and it is these, above all, which help us to enter the sphere of the Word and the Spirit. These factors bring a tremendous spiritual dynamic to our communication.

Spiritual memory

The power of spiritual memory is vital to our Christian communication. In his book *The Ministry of God's Word*, Watchman Nee highlights the necessity of understanding what this means. He says:

> 'Another thing of which a minister of the word must take note is memory, the power to remember. It occupies a much larger place in ministry than we usually think. We have much to learn in this respect...'

> 'We can only say what we remember, not what we do not remember. How does the inward word uphold the spoken word? How does the former flow out? Without the support of the inward word there will be no spoken word. If the inward word is absent, the spoken word must change its subject, for the subject is in the inward word and not in the spoken word. The second needs the backing of the first, or else it will wither away. Here then is the significance of memory. It is through recall that the inward word is transported to the outside ... A strange experience common to all the ministers of the word is that the more you remember doctrine the less you recall revelation. You may understand teaching, be quite clear on it, and remember it well. But with revelation it is different ... The memory we need is of two kinds: the outward memory and the Holy Spirit memory. A minister of the word needs both. The outward memory points to the memory of the outward man, that which is produced in a man's brain. It occupies a

very important place in testifying the word of God. The Holy Spirit memory is what the Lord Jesus mentions in John 14.26: "But the Helper, the Holy Spirit, whom the Father will send in my name, He will teach you all things, and bring to your remembrance all that I said to you." This is Holy Spirit memory, for it is the Holy Spirit who brings to your remembrance, not you yourself.'

Nee expresses this in his own unique way but I believe he is putting into words what many of us who are preachers know intuitively. More than that, we can identify the sorts of areas where this empowering of the Holy Spirit makes all the difference between our words coming out full of spiritual power and being an empty sound with no saving virtue.

Let's take a look at some important areas where this principle might be proved true:

Scriptures

It is not so difficult to memorize Scripture at the level of the outward man, neither is it difficult to repeat Scriptures at this level. The recollection and repetition of Scriptures for their own sakes is not a guarantee that what we say will flow with power into the lives of our hearers. A deeper level of recollection must be reached. When Scripture is quoted it must not be by rote or just for the sake of a useful illustration of the point in hand. There needs to be a recollection in the power of the Holy Spirit. In other words, the words of Scripture must be brought back through us from the inside to the outside with all the life and power of the Spirit of God. When this happens, we, as well as our listeners will feel the innate power of the recalled word of Scripture.

Testimonies

Another dimension of our use of memory is when we have something to say out of our experience. Testimony of an occasion, perhaps, when God really spoke in a personal and powerful way; when we grasped light concerning a truth that we'd never really seen before. Forgive a personal example, but every time I quote the opening verses of Isaiah 6, I know the reality of this experience. Not only does it fulfil what we have already considered about the living reality of God's word coming through. For me, it also recalls the greatest testimony in my own life of the breakthrough of the holy power and majesty of the living God.

It is not only that the words themselves vibrate with power, it is as though the Spirit of God helps me to re-live the sensation of the experience in a way that breaks through into the inmost hearts of those who listen.

> *'In the year that King Uzziah died I saw the Lord seated on a throne, and the train of his robe filled the temple. Above him were seraphs, each with six wings: With two wings they covered their faces, with two they covered their feet, and with two they were flying. And they were calling to one another:*
> *"Holy, holy, holy is the Lord Almighty; the whole earth is full of his glory." '*

These are amazing words – yet they're only words, great though they are. I once had an experience of God. It was different from Isaiah in the sense that I wasn't in a temple, I didn't live 600 years before Jesus and I wasn't a Jew. This, however, is the only part of the Bible that comes near to describing the experience I had in the Spirit that day. I understood, not only with my mind, but deep in my inner being, what Isaiah meant. Now I only preach from Isaiah 6 when there is another movement in my spirit of the same ilk. When I feel a personal, powerful, spiritual recollection. Not just remembering about the occasion, but reliving it.

This is something that all preachers need to learn. We must ask the Holy Spirit to help us to relive our testimonies. If I stand up to tell people and I don't have my spiritual memory in operation; if what happened inside the event doesn't live again, then what I say will not have the same effect. I am convinced that if we can live and speak in the power of this spiritual recall then we will begin to get to the heart of really powerful person-to-person communication.

Illustrations

An illustration helps people to live in the reality of which you speak; it brings truth to life. However, whilst it can be terrific as an enabler, it can be awful as a master. It is essential that you avoid stories that become hackneyed and old hat. As I've already mentioned, at theological college we were taught to collect and collate every useful illustration and quotation. The intention was that these would be to hand when the time came to fill out the sermon with suitable notes, quotes and anecdotes.

It seems hard to believe that one of the most fluent and lively of all English preachers, used to advise his students to buy a good book of sermon outlines and anecdotes to sustain them throughout their ministries. My experience has been that if material has mostly been second-hand to begin with it is unlikely that it will be first-hand for those who receive it from us. However, whether our illustrations are culled and collected like this or not, we need to go far beyond this in our communication of them to other people. Here too we need to develop a spiritual memory. Ask God to quicken your memory. I have found that the Holy Spirit will lodge many illustrations from the daily experience of life, some of which may go quite unnoticed at the time but later, when the Spirit of God brings it to mind with power for the sake of clothing the point with life it comes with such clarity and vitality that it enhances the truth with power.

Illustration can come very powerfully through a vision in the mind. If you can interpret what you receive from God with this vision or picture, you'll find that someone sitting out there in front of you knows precisely at a technical or practical level what you're talking about. I once had a remarkable experience in Burundi, Central Africa. I was preaching in an evangelistic meeting with thousands of people and suddenly a picture came into my mind. It was of a great big concrete conduit. The sort of pipe that goes under a road to carry water, for example. As I was preaching this picture persisted in my mind. I had to firmly resist the thought that the picture could not be from the Holy Spirit because in the middle of Africa this sort of conduit would be unknown. However, the picture kept rising in my mind so powerfully, that I proceeded to use the illustration. When the people of Burundi appreciate something, they make what sounds like a sucking noise behind their front teeth. As I gave the illustration there was a sound from these five thousand people that resembled a very large congregation of hens enjoying their grain! I was amazed that it seemed so effective. After the meeting I discovered that the government had just started to build a new road in a certain part of town and for the first time the local people saw the big concrete pipes being put under the road to carry water through. Instead of being something that we take for granted, it was so exciting to these people. One week they saw it for the first time, the next week the preacher is using it as an illustration of how God channels His power in to our lives. That's spiritual vision.

Release of power

When our spiritual memory causes our words to have living reality then there is that 'discharge' of power as Watchman Nee calls it. When you live in your experience, through the power of the Holy Spirit, then what happens is that other people start to live in it with you. Real preaching and teaching is about the intermingling of two wonderful releases from God – the release of the Holy Spirit and the release of the power of the word of God.

The Final Word

Today the question often arises about what follows the preaching. Should there be some sort of personal ministry? Perhaps a time of prayer to seal the word and draw out a response from the hearers.

With many preachers of a past generation this was never a question. The thought of following up the spoken word with anything else would never have entered their heads. The word of God was held to be effective by itself. The only exceptions were evangelistic meetings in which an opportunity might be given for people to respond if they felt the Lord had spoken to them. Now it is taken for granted in many contexts that ministry of prayer and/or the laying-on of hands, or some other personal ministry will follow the declaration of the word. Maybe the pendulum has swung too far the other way because I am sure we need the discernment of the Spirit of God to show us what is appropriate after the spoken word. I am sure there are times when it is quite wrong to add anything else to the word which people have received in their hearts. We must never feel bound by the traditions or expectations of people to do anything – unless God directs it. Then, of course, it would be just as wrong to ignore the leading of the Spirit and miss the opportunity to bring the saving and healing power of God to the people through other ministry.

As far as the New Testament is concerned the manifestation of signs and wonders was present from the very beginning of the proclamation of the Kingdom and is the normal corollary to the proclamation of the word.

> 'This salvation, which was first announced by the Lord, was confirmed to us by those who heard him. God also testified to it by signs, wonders and various miracles, and gifts of the Holy Spirit distributed according to his will.'
> (Hebrews 2:3, 4)

Perhaps the following four simple, practical rules might be helpful:

(1) **Always be open to the possibility of further ministry.** Although we must never be browbeaten by false expectations, likewise we must also be open to the possibility that we may have to follow up the spoken word with

some other spiritual ministry. This is when the wider range of spiritual gifts comes into operation. When we are ministering we will find that words of knowledge, the gifts of discernment, healing, faith, deliverance of spirits and the like all come into play. These are all 'back-up' gifts to the Word of God. It is good that so many have been opened up to the operation of spiritual gifts of power today.

(2) **Be sensitive to the occasion.** Every occasion demands a different approach. One of the dangers of getting into fixed attitudes concerning ministry is that things may be imposed on a situation that are totally inappropriate. There are some occasions which call for ministry and others that don't. It's part of the preacher's job to develop an inward sensitivity to what would be appropriate to any particular situation. We can learn this from the ministry of Jesus. He was always sensitive to whether there was faith present or not. On some occasions He could do no mighty deeds because of the unbelief of the people. Some of us wouldn't have the sense to assess the spiritual atmosphere. We just plough on and then end up devastated. Giving out the power of God into a situation that doesn't warrant it, will expose the minister to a negative repercussion in spirit. We need to be open to the leading of the Holy Spirit.

(3) **Don't be bullied by other people.** Some audiences, groups or organisations have already worked out the format of the programme in great detail. They expect every speaker to follow their rules to the letter. This opens up the possibility of a tension between the in-built expectations of the audience and the sensitivities of one's own spirit. Experience has taught me that it is better to make clear at the start, perhaps even before accepting the invitation to speak, what one's own grounds of action are likely to be. This can prevent tension from arising and takes away the further possibility of unnecessary embarrassment.

(4) **Never detract from the word of God.** Whatever happens, nothing must detract from the word of God. The word of God is what will endure. We must be careful not to let an emotion of the moment rob people of the word which God has planted in them. None of this is in any way to deny the need and the possibility of spiritual ministry. It is necessary, however, to redress the balance somewhat in an age where ministry has become everything for some people, and the depths and power of God's word alone has been discarded.

I am convinced that we are entering a day when the word of God will be seen for what it is – the word of God, full of power. I am also convinced that we need to get away from the idea that it is men that bring this ministry. Paul got it right when he declared that we do not preach ourselves, but Christ Jesus as Lord. Whatever the mechanism of ministry it needs to leave people face to face with Jesus and with the living power of God.

Challenges

Over my years as a preacher and teacher, I can recall two things in particular that have really challenged me. Many years ago, before videos were commonplace, the Church Pastoral Aid Society within the Church of England published a film strip on Evangelism. The title was one of those titles I have always wished I'd thought of first. It was called – 'It's not what you say, it's what they hear'. This is the real challenge of communication. Recently I was challenged in a similar way by something else I heard: 'They have to hear, but they don't have to listen'. Our challenge as preachers, teachers and communicators is to present the word in the power of God so that some transaction will take place in our hearers which will cause them to listen; perhaps as they have never done in their lives before.

James Stewart in his book *Heralds of God* tells the story of an event that took place during the 1914–18 war. In France, one cold winter day, some men went to listen to a Roman

Catholic priest. Their expectations were zero. They expected something dry as dust, but what happened was entirely different. They met in a cellar. The old priest came in and sat down on the floor and they all sat around him. He was struggling for words, obviously profoundly affected by something in his spirit. He didn't know how to communicate the depth of what was in him, yet he sat for an hour and from his innermost being he spoke to them about the Scripture *'Come unto Me all ye that labour and are heavy laden and I will give you rest.'* One man reported afterwards that 'for one hour not a man moved a muscle.'

James Stewart comments 'There you have a striking example of the power of preaching – to mediate the real presence of God in Jesus Christ.'

Paul says in Colossians 1:28, 29:

> *'We proclaim Him, admonishing and teaching everyone with all wisdom, so that we may present everyone perfect in Christ. To this end I labour, struggling with all His energy, which so powerfully works in me.'*

This is true spiritual communication. May God release such preaching and teaching into the Body of Christ today, to the glory of His holy Name. Amen.

References

1. Stormont, George. 1990. *Smith Wigglesworth: A Man Who Walked With God.* Sovereign World

Heralds of God

The essence of the book you have just read is available in the form of two exciting and useful video recordings called *Heralds of God*.

Heralds of God is made up of two videos each with four teaching sessions, eight sessions in all. Each session deals with one major aspect of the subject of spiritual communication. These videos contain not only important spiritual insights but a great deal of practical help.

These videos are of great value, not only for individual use, but also for group study and training sessions. They are designed to be of particular use in stimulating and developing the gifts of preaching and teaching in the Body of Christ today.

Heralds of God is available by mail order from Kerygma International Christian Ministries, The Christian Life Centre, Drayton Hall, Hall Lane, Drayton, Norwich, UK, NR8 6DP. Other publications and videos by Dr Bob Gordon are available from the same address. List on request.

01603 260222

If you have enjoyed this book and would like to help us to send a copy of it and many other titles to needy pastors in the **Third World**, please write for further information or send your gift to:

Sovereign World Trust
PO Box 777, Tonbridge
Kent TN11 9XT
United Kingdom

or to the **'Sovereign World'** distributor in your country.

If sending money from outside the United Kingdom, please send an International Money Order or Foreign Bank Draft in STERLING, drawn on a **UK** bank to **Sovereign World Trust**.